UNCOMFORTABLE CONVERSATIONS WITH A BLACK MAN

UNCOMFORTABLE CONVERSATIONS WITH A BLACK MAN

Emmanuel Acho

FLATIRON
BOOKS
NEW YORK

UNCOMFORTABLE CONVERSATIONS WITH A BLACK MAN. Copyright ©
2020 by EA Enterprises, LLC. All rights reserved. Printed in the
United States of America. For information, address Flatiron Books,
120 Broadway, New York, NY 10271.

Grateful acknowledgment is made for permission to reproduce from the
following:

Excerpts of "I Am a Black" and "A Primer for Blacks" by Gwendolyn
Brooks reprinted by consent of Brooks Permissions.

www.flatironbooks.com

Designed by Jonathan Bennett

The Library of Congress has cataloged the hardcover edition as follows:

Names: Acho, Emmanuel, author.
Title: Uncomfortable conversations with a black man / Emmanuel Acho.
Description: First edition. | New York : Flatiron Books, 2020.
Identifiers: LCCN 2020946015 | ISBN 9781250800466 (hardcover) |
    ISBN 9781250800480 (ebook)
LC record available at https://lccn.loc.gov/2020946015

ISBN 978-1-250-80047-3 (trade paperback)

Our books may be purchased in bulk for promotional, educational, or
business use. Please contact your local bookseller or the Macmillan
Corporate and Premium Sales Department at 1-800-221-7945, extension
5442, or by email at MacmillanSpecialMarkets@macmillan.com.

First Flatiron Books Paperback Edition: 2021

10 9 8 7 6 5 4 3 2 1

To those who marched, kneeled,
and hoped in faith

...those who entered, thomas
mgh1 rob that

CONTENTS

INTRODUCTION

Dear white friends, countrypersons: welcome. Pull up a chair.

Consider this book an invitation to the table. It's a special table—but don't worry, this isn't one of those uptight, where's-your-VIP-reservation places, rather a come-as-you-are joint for my white brothers and sisters and anyone else inclined to join us. The room where this table sits is a safe space, by which I mean a space to learn things you've always wondered about, a place where questions you may have been afraid to ask get answered. For all of you who lack an honest black friend in your life, consider me that friend.

My arms are open wide, friends. My heart, too.

Before I get into more of what to expect from the book, I want to share a few things about myself. I've been navigating the lines between whiteness and blackness all of my life—starting with growing up in Dallas, Texas, as the son of Nigerian immigrants.

My homelife was steeped in Nigerian culture, rather than black American culture; I only got that on Sundays and on Wednesdays at church. My surroundings, meanwhile, were disproportionately white, from my upper-class suburban neighborhood to the private school I was fortunate to attend. I became "Manny" to all the kids who decided my real name was too foreign.

I wasn't unaware of racism, growing up. My home state, as you may know, is the birthplace of Juneteenth, a holiday that celebrates the day enslaved people in Texas discovered they'd been set free—the last group of black people to find out. It's a day that, among other things, calls attention to the state's long Confederate history. There might not have been any Lost Cause soldiers terrorizing my neighborhood, but from the time I was nine or ten years old, I knew I'd experienced racism. It wasn't that overt, call-you-the-N-word-to-your-face racism. It was more subtle. Like, for example, the uncountable times some kid in elementary school or middle school or high school plopped down at my lunch table and, after hearing me recount some playground feat, said, "You don't even talk like you're black," or "You don't sound black," or "You don't even dress like you're black." Or the ever-popular "You're like an Oreo: black on the outside, white on the inside."

I was offended, but I also thought—*Maybe they're right? Maybe I'm not black enough? Thank you if you're telling me I sound smart . . . but then, are you saying black people can't be smart?* Let me tell you, kid Emmanuel was working on an identity complex.

You should've seen me when I got to the University of Texas and found myself surrounded by more black people than I ever had been. *Yo,* I realized, *these are my people.* I'm home at last. You know when Tarzan finally met some humans and was like, "Oh, I'm a *human*"? It was like that. Those early college years were the first time I understood what it means to be a black man in America. Part of this meant realizing how my childhood had given me misguided impressions about my own people. I had been fed the same stereotypical stuff about black people as the white kids around me, and I hadn't been immune: they had me under the impression that the only *real* way to be black was to be Nelly circa 2002, minus the Band-Aid under the eye. Finally surrounded by so many different expressions of blackness, I knew I was fine the way I was. But I started to wonder: If I, a first-generation-American black man, could be taught to believe distorted things in such a short time, how much easier is it for a white person to believe them?

Today, I'm grateful for all my experiences, because they were all a kind of lesson. Ask anybody: to be fluent in a language, you have to study abroad. I studied Spanish all four years of high school, but I was never fluent because I never set foot in Spain. Well, my childhood was one big study abroad in white culture—followed by studying abroad in black culture during college and then during my years in the NFL, which I spent on teams with 80–90 percent black players, each of whom had his own experience of being a person of color in America. Now, I'm fluent in both cultures: black and white.

The book you're reading is what I want to do with that perspective.

WE'RE IN THE MIDST of the greatest pandemic in recent times, which has the potential to be the greatest pandemic of all time. (Friends, wear your masks and wash your hands.) However, the longest-lasting pandemic in this country is a virus not of the body but of the mind, and it's called racism. I'm not sure if we can cure racism completely, but I also believe that as we rush to find a vaccine for COVID-19, we should be pursuing with equal determination a cure for the virus of racism and oppression. "The ultimate logic of racism," Martin Luther King Jr. once said, "is genocide." I don't mean to be the Bad News Bears, but we are living in an America that necessitated the Black Lives Matter movement. A country in which the simple declaration that *people who look like me are worth saving* has become controversial.

Enough. I want to be a catalyst for change, to help cure the systemic injustices that have led to the tragic deaths of too many of my brothers and sisters; prisons popping up like fast-food chains; inequalities in health care and education; the forced facts of who gets to live where; the ingrained ignorance of Americans who can't see beyond skin color. I believe an important part of the cure, maybe the most crucial part of it, is to talk to each other.

Let me take a second to break down what I mean. I don't mean chatting about whatever; I mean a two-way dialogue based on trust and respect, full of information exchanged and perspectives shared. The goal here is to build relationships—and, ultimately, to help us recognize each other's humanity. I'd bet some Dallas Cowboys season tickets that it's tough, if not impossible, to hold bigoted thoughts about someone whose humanity you recognize. I'd double down: it would take some next-level self-deluding to discriminate against someone you respect enough to listen to.

IN THESE PAGES, the only bad question is the unasked question. You'll see that each chapter starts with a question, each of which is from a real email I've received in response to my video series. (Same title as this book, if you got here without watching.) I appreciate every one of them, because wherever the askers are coming from, they came to learn.

If things go the way I want, you will leave this book with an increased understanding of race. You will have more empathy and grant people more grace. And if you have more empathy and are more gracious, then you'll be less judgmental. And if you're less judgmental, then your judgment is less likely to play itself out in racism.

Now, there are degrees of racism. If you're reading this, I imagine you're not a white-hood-wearing, Confederate-statue-defending, *Dukes of Hazzard*–idolizing, tiki-torch-toting, N-word-barking first-degree racist. However, you might fall between the second or third degree, meaning someone who is not overtly racist but is on a spectrum between a person who is a little racially insensitive or ignorant and someone who holds deeply ingrained negative ideas about people of other races and ethnicities. Even if none of the above descriptions fit you, you might know someone they do fit.

PAUSE—DID THAT MAKE you uncomfortable to read? Look, I won't lie to you, we're only getting further in the weeds from here. We're going to talk about slavery a lot. We're going to talk about privilege. And complicity. And so on.

BUT: getting uncomfortable is the whole idea. Everything great is birthed through discomfort. Think about it—a mother suffers no small amount of trouble for nine months before enduring the mega-pain of labor in birthing the world's next great hero genius. I endured years and years of grueling football practices, many of them under a scorching Texas sun, before I made it to the NFL. Most of our major accomplishments are accompanied by some form of discomfort.

If we truly want to treat this four-hundred-year-old American virus that has been doing its work since the first stolen Africans landed in Jamestown in 1619, then we are all going to have to buckle in.

Before we get this thing going, a couple of caveats from me. I don't profess to know everything about black culture, or to speak for every black experience in this country. I'm aware that I move through the world as a man (down with the patriarchy), that I've lived in affluent neighborhoods, and that I attended a private school growing up. Add to that the fact that I'm from a home of first-generation immigrants, which is a different experience from a black person whose family has been in America for generations. All told, mine is a particular perspective. That said: I am a black man in this country. I have been walking around in this skin all my life, interacting with black (and white) people for all my twenty-nine years. What I can do is tell you how it looks from here.

IN HIS POEM "Let America Be America Again," Langston Hughes writes, "O, let America be America Again / The land that never has been yet." Hughes published these words in 1936, almost twenty years before the civil rights movement, a time when he had strong reason to critique America for not fulfilling its promise. At the time of the 1965 march across the Edmund Pettus Bridge in Selma, Alabama, a large swath of white people were unwilling to make America what it could be. At the time of the 1992 LA uprising, scores of white people were still resistant to forging a version of America that made good on its founding principles. In 2016, when Colin Kaepernick started kneeling, white America showed that they were dramatically divided on accepting how far America still has to go. Now it's 2020: more than eight decades after Langston's poem. In the wake of the devastating murder of George Floyd, I believe the majority of white Americans are now ready to help America become the land it dreamed for itself.

It's going to take all of us—you, me, everybody—to achieve the dream. You are going to have to learn how to move beyond being *not* racist, to being *anti*racist (a term that's been around for decades, but was recently made popular by scholar Ibram X. Kendi). If you're reading these words, I'm going to venture that you are ready to see an America that the great Langston Hughes challenged us all to will into existence. Huddle up, my friends. It starts with an uncomfortable conversation.

Thank you for listening, sharing, and believing. Let's change the world—together.

Part I

YOU
AND ME

"How do you bring race up with minorities? I honestly have so much fear of saying something wrong and being labeled as a 'racist.' I'm sure things will come out wrong, or sound unaware because they are. But how will I learn if we can't discuss?" —Melissa

1.

THE NAME GAME

Black or African American?

> According to my Teachers,
> I am now an African-American.
> They call me out of my name.
> BLACK is an open umbrella.
> I am a Black and A Black forever.
> I am one of The Blacks.
>
> —GWENDOLYN BROOKS, "I AM A BLACK"

On June 5, 2020, in Washington, D.C., city workers painted three bold words down the street leading directly to the White House: BLACK LIVES MATTER. The city had already renamed this section of D.C.'s Sixteenth Street to Black Lives Matter Plaza, and now they had a two-block-long street mural so big you could see it from space. Size matters, but the heart of the mural is the language, and the key word here is this one: black.

We'll get (way) further into the Black Lives Matter movement, but for now, let's keep it real: "African American lives matter!" as a motto just doesn't have the same ring to it.

Giant murals aside, what do you call a person of African descent living in America: black, African American, colored, Negro? (Okay, I was just playing about the last two. Those terms have been dead.) Does it matter what you call us? I want to start with this question because I get it a lot, and if we're going to have a good, long conversation, first I want you to know how I identify myself. I also want to start here because definitions are going to be important throughout this book—the words we use have power, especially around race. And none of them, these included, are simple.

Let's Rewind

HISTORICALLY AND PRESENTLY, black people have a hard time agreeing on how to describe ourselves as a group. We must never forget that the lion's share of people of African descent living in this country had ancestors that were seized from their homeland and stripped of the core parts of their identities: kinship ties, links to a tribe, language, and so on. That they suffered a hellish journey. That when they reached the shores of what became America, they became something less than human—legally—and were deprived of the most important things that made them, them.

We must never lose sight of the fact that this torture went on for hundreds of years, until the end of the Civil War, and even beyond it (remember what I said about Juneteenth).*

As part of establishing themselves after the Civil War, emancipated black people began to adopt different racial labels. The first widely used term was *colored*, because it was accepted by both white and black people and deemed inclusive of those who had mixed racial ancestry, too. *Colored* reigned supreme into the early twentieth century and can still be found in the name of what might be the most important black organization of all time: the NAACP (the National Association for the Advancement of Colored People, founded in 1909).

The rise of progressive black figures like Booker T. Washington and W. E. B. Du Bois spurred a shift from *colored* to *Negro* as the dominant term. Du Bois pitched *Negro* as philosophically stronger and also as more versatile since it could be used as a noun or an adjective. *Negro* held on for a few decades, from

---

* This isn't gonna be a footnote book, but I want to say this up front: while sometimes on TV I might use the term *slave*, in this book, I've been careful to use the word *en*slaved to describe black people who were forced into bondage. There is a big difference between *slave* and *enslaved*. Calling someone a slave is like saying that's what they *were*: like they were born into this identity, like what's happening to them is in line with who they are. *En*slaved, on the other hand, puts emphasis on what happened. *Enslaved* says black people weren't naturally born as slaves: they were coerced into slavery. *Enslaved* puts the emphasis on what white people did to black people.

the early twentieth century until the end of the civil rights movement. One of the chief arguments against *Negro* eventually gained the upper hand: that it was originally a term imposed by white people onto black people.

After the late 1960s, *black* came into its own. One of the main arguments for using *black* was that it created a parallel with white. (Which, side note, is also an invented term—European immigrants didn't arrive here saying, "White and proud"!) *Black* birthed phrases like "black and beautiful," "Black and Proud," and groups like the Black Muslims and Black Panthers, and generally dominated through the 1970s and into the '80s.

Then, in 1988, black leaders met in Chicago to discuss the "National Black Agenda," where some of them proposed replacing *black* with *African-American*. One of those leaders was activist and former presidential candidate Jesse Jackson. (Right, Obama was not the first to run.) Jackson explained his group's thinking: "Just as we were called colored, but were not that, and then Negro, but not that, to be called black is just as baseless. Every ethnic group in this country has reference to some cultural base. African Americans have hit that level of maturity." Those advocating for the use of *African-American* over *black* criticized *black* as a label that was originally assigned by slave owners and also highlighted the links between black and sin, between black and dishonesty, between black and a lack of virtue, between black and a whole bunch of negative connotations. *African-American*, they argued, instead celebrated a cultural heritage.

Not everyone was on board with the switch—including Gwendolyn Brooks, whose poem "I Am a Black" started this chapter. Brooks, the first black person to win a Pulitzer Prize (1950), published a whole collection of poems called *Blacks* in 1973. Among other things, she liked how inclusive "black" was, an "open umbrella" for anyone with skin like hers. Others opposed to Jackson and his shift to *African-American* argued that its hyphenation was another way of subjugating black people: a.k.a. you're not *American* Americans, you're this subset. Still others felt that all the name-changing business was a diversion that drew attention away from the real problems. (Ironically, some Black Lives Matter advocates criticized the mayor of D.C. for the huge mural, calling it a distraction from their goals of police reform.)

So that's where we are, history-wise. There remain camps of those who favor *black* and those who favor *African American* (pretty sure *Negro* and *colored* won't be making any comebacks, but one never knows). You may also have heard the term *POC* or *BIPOC*—People of Color or Black Indigenous People of Color. Rather than a synonym for *black*, this is more a synonym for *minority*, once the go-to for anyone nonwhite. I prefer it to *minority*, for the record, because people of color make up the global majority!

Let's Get Uncomfortable

I IMAGINE SOME of you are thinking: If black people can't decide which term to use, then how and why should white people be expected to know which term to use? Point taken. But all that means is that this conversation is worth having.

I've had my own journey. Growing up, at home, I felt Nigerian, because that's what my family was— but out in the world, I felt black, because I knew that's how the rest of the world saw me. I knew this despite the fact that, as I said in the intro, I wasn't even sure I knew what being black meant . . . like, was I black enough if I was listening to R&B instead of Lil Wayne or Nas? Whatever I doubted about the specifics, my skin color made me a lifetime member of the club.

As for African American, no one embodies the definition more than I do. Even as I'm now immersed in black American culture, I'm actually a dual citizen of the United States and Nigeria, and I go back to my father's home village for a few weeks every year (on medical mission work). Still, I don't personally identify with the term *African American*. If you're gonna go there, I mean, get it right—I'm Nigerian American. I'm not from the whole continent.

To the extent I can speak for anyone else: black is the most inclusive choice. Here's Gwendolyn Brooks again, this time from her poem "Primer for Blacks":

The word Black
has geographic power,
pulls everybody in:
Blacks here—
Blacks there—
Blacks wherever they may be.

BLACK COVERS THE descendants of the people who were brought over on slave ships and forced to work on plantations and also includes people like my parents, who immigrated to the United States. It covers all the black people in the United States and also joins them with people of African descent in Brazil, the Caribbean, Mexico (the diaspora), and other countries where the transatlantic slave trade brought Africans. It's a descriptor of what black people all have in common.

There's no one label that will satisfy all (who knows, maybe there's some old head who still wants to be called *Negro*), but there is usually an opportunity to ask someone their preference. Yes, it might be uncomfortable, but it's the right thing to do. It's also a decision that will keep you from making mistakes, from offending someone when that's not your intent.

Talk It, Walk It

WELL INFORMED. WE'VE all got to be as well informed as we can be. And to that end, I suggest reading writer

Tom Smith's essay "Changing Racial Labels: From 'Colored' to 'Negro' to 'Black' to 'African American.'" And check out Kee Malesky's "The Journey from 'Colored' to 'Minorities' to 'People of Color,'" published on npr.org.

And when in doubt—again, just ask. Remember in school, when a new teacher would ask if anyone had a particular way of saying their name or even went by another name? Jennifer would say she wanted to be called Jen. Some guy named Fernando said he preferred going by Flip. Jonathan Jr. wanted to be called JJ. And the teacher, if they cared, marked those names in the roll book, and that was that. They didn't question why the students had those preferences, they just respected them. The question of whether to use *black* or *African American* is ultimately a preference, one that helps a person present their identity to the world. Each person you meet might not have a preference, but maybe they do. Trust me, language matters.

"What are some of the best ways to find and get rid of your implicit bias?"—Patrick

2.

WHAT DO YOU SEE WHEN YOU SEE ME?

Implicit Bias

Prejudice is an emotional commitment
to ignorance.

—NATHAN RUTSTEIN

B ack in 2015, Google's rollout of its Photos app ran into a big, racist problem. The app had a feature that suggested tags for objects and people, distinguishing each with coding to "recognize" faces. One user, a black computer programmer named Jacky Alciné, found a serious bug: the app kept tagging him and his girlfriend as "gorillas."

Alciné tweeted the error at Google, which got him a swift "This is 100% Not OK" from the company's chief social architect. The tag itself might seem funny until you remember that black people were long insulted as "apes" and "monkeys" and, yes, "gorillas"—all ways of saying "less than human." Now, assuming Google's engineers weren't trying to add a racist Easter egg to their Photos app: Why was this happening? Why weren't white people being tagged as polar bears?

The short answer is that the facial recognition algorithm had been disproportionately coded to, and tested on, white faces. It didn't recognize black faces because no one had thought to teach it to do so.

The long answer is something called *implicit bias*.

Let me first point out that everyone has implicit biases, including me. They're not just about race—they're your knee-jerk judgments about every superficial difference between people. And don't get me wrong: you shouldn't beat yourself up for every single biased thought or decision. If you see a clown and think, *DANGER*, look, you're not the only one. At the same time, you're responsible for your biases, if for no other reason than that there are ways to make them more conscious. And when an idea is conscious, you can change your mind.

Let's Rewind

IN A 2016 article titled "Whitened Résumés: Race and Self-Preservation in the Labor Market," professors from Harvard, Stanford, and the University of

Toronto reported on a two-year study about the effect of people of color using whitewashed names on their résumés. ("Lamar J. Smith" became "L. James Smith," etc.) I'll give you one wild guess what the researchers discovered. Yup: applicants with white-sounding names were more likely to be called back for an interview. And not just by a little bit. They were almost *twice* as likely to be called back.

Adding insult to injury, the research showed that companies advertising themselves as pro-diversity discriminated just as much, and sometimes even more! This is exhibit A of implicit bias: when a company thinks of itself as an "equal opportunity employer," or goes out of its way to say, "Minorities are strongly encouraged to apply," they may be lying and *not even realize it*. Black applicants get the false confidence that it's A-OK to reveal their race on their résumés and then, boom, catch a biased rejection, while pro-diversity company X wonders why they still have so few "diverse" employees.

As you probably know by now, what someone says is not necessarily a good gauge of the whole of what they think or feel, nor how they'll behave. Anyone can act on biases—prejudice and stereotypes—without being aware that's what they are doing. But as with "equal opportunity" employers, once bias informs our thinking, it can lead to explicit racism and bigotry.

Some of the most popular recent baby names for

black boys and girls are Jevonte, Kyrone, Tamika, and Shantel. I'm willing to bet these names wouldn't have fared well in the above study. And one might say, it's just a callback for an interview—but think about all the things that can happen as a result of being *half* as likely to get that callback. That means longer periods of unemployment. More unemployment means a greater risk of homelessness. Think about what joblessness does to a person's esteem, to their mental health. Think about the fact that with no job, there's likely no health insurance or no good health insurance. And what about feeling like your name is the cause of your life's troubles?

Are you starting to see how damaging a knee-jerk reaction can be?

Implicit bias on the job is just one source of fallout. It's also common elsewhere. Ever heard of "driving while black"? Or how hard it can be for black people to catch a cab? These are old clichés for a reason—black people get pulled over way more often than white people and have to deal every day with the kind of snap judgment a taxi driver makes. These little slights happen constantly, and they're exhausting.

In hospitals, bias can literally determine whether a person lives or dies. According to *Eliminating Racial Disparities in Maternal and Infant Mortality*, a 2019 report published by the Center for American Progress, black women across the income spectrum and from all walks of life are dying from preventable pregnancy-related complications at three to four times—I REPEAT: THREE TO FOUR TIMES!—the rate of non-Hispanic white women. The death rate for black infants is twice that of infants born to non-Hispanic white mothers.

If we assume the doctors and nurses of this nation mean well, what's going on? Black women have long been thought capable of bearing more physical pain, have received less careful, attentive, thorough health care, and have failed to be treated with dignity by health care professionals. Those factors create a chain of biological processes known as *weathering* that undermines black women's physical and mental health. It is literally killing their babies. And a major reason for why it's happening is implicit bias.

Don't get it twisted—saying these disparities are due to bias isn't a way out of saying they're due to racism. Again, unconscious prejudices can manifest as racist actions, that's the whole problem. But I think it's important to start here, with the fact that you don't even have to know you're racist for the damage to be done.

Let's Get Uncomfortable

WHAT ARE YOUR implicit biases against black people and people of other races? How have those biases played out in your decision-making, in how you treat people?

I'll go first. I did track and field way back when,

and I still love a good track meet. So I was watching the Texas High School Championships last year, and we got to the one hundred meter finals. The eight lanes were filled up with the black kids I expected to see—all except lane four. "Matthew Boling?" Who was this lanky white dude? I knew he was the favorite, because lane four is always reserved for the fastest seed, but my mind instantly went back to the joke-not-joke the black sprinters on my team had: "Don't let the white kid beat you."

Sure enough, this kid Boling ended up setting the meet record, tying the Texas state record for the one hundred meters. Touché, my white friend.

I'm sure talking about these things is uncomfortable for many of you. Especially for those of you who believe yourself to be a good person, who don't consider yourself a racist, who want to treat people fairly. But that's all the more reason to discuss your biases, to learn about them, critique them, to try to trace where they come from. I like to use the acronym DENIAL: Don't Even kNow I Am Lying. The first way to end racism is for my white counterparts to get out of denial, to understand that, wait a second, maybe you've been lying to yourself about the existence of racism this whole time. You need a counter voice in your head when you notice your internal monologue ushering you toward making a biased decision or judgment against black people. Everyone, and I mean everyone, has biases. It's the job of empathetic and considerate people not to let them dictate actions that harm others.

Talk It, Walk It

"LOTS OF WORK being done, and lots still to be done," tweeted Yonatan Zunger, chief architect of social at Google in 2015. "We're very much on it." After trying and failing to fix the algorithm that labeled black people as gorillas, the company removed the gorilla label altogether. They're still working on a better way to recognize the full spectrum of human faces. Therein lies a lesson for those of us who are not billion-dollar tech giants: it can be easier to avoid bad PR than to fix the root problem.

In order for us to conquer our implicit biases, we have to speak openly and honestly about them. Uncomfortable conversation is all about addressing this kind of thinking, airing it out. We can't let these ideas fester in silence.

So, what's a game plan for reducing implicit biases?

One way is to spend time with people in different social, racial, and ethnic groups. You can do things like join meetups, join a gym or fitness class, take a class in something you're interested in, drop by a new desk at work, walk around your neighborhood, or even just sit down in one of those often-empty bus or subway seats next to a black man and strike up a conversation. The more you reach out, the easier it gets, I promise.

Another way is to stop celebrating "color blindness." HGTV stars Chip and Joanna Gaines came on my show earlier this year and told me that one day they asked their kids to pretend they saw two strangers, a black man and a white man. Would the black man make them more nervous? The kids all said no, really quickly, and the Gaineses took that as evidence that their kids were color blind—that they didn't "see race." Was that a good thing, they asked? Answer: it's actually not. Not only does that overlook the difference between the experience of being a black versus a white person in this country (more on that . . . throughout this book), it also provides a fertile ground for implicit biases to grow unrecognized and unchecked.

Instead of being color blind, be introspective. Try to identify your prejudices and hold them up to scrutiny. If you don't know what they are, you can start by taking an implicit bias test. (Here's one: https://implicit.harvard.edu/implicit/takeatest.html.) Pay special attention to your biases when you're stressed, as that's when they are more likely to pop up without you noticing. As much as you can, try to imagine you're me—consider things from the perspective of someone you know is susceptible to discrimination or stereotyping.

Avoid lumping people into groups in general. Meet your peers as individuals. Affirm people's particularities and differences. That's what makes us human.

In your job, your school, or any other institution you belong to, be supportive of measures to diversify—along with measures of accountability. It's like riding the New York subway: if you see something, say something.

"Do you believe that, with time, white privilege can be eliminated? Also, when I think about white privilege, I feel guilty and ashamed." —Maria

3.

THE FALSE START
White Privilege

Race doesn't really exist for you because it has never been a barrier. Black folks don't have that choice.

—CHIMAMANDA NGOZI ADICHIE, *AMERICANAH*

Say you and I are in a race and the starting line official held me back for the first two hundred meters, giving you a two-hundred-meter head start. If that were to happen, the only way to level out that race would be to either stop you from running or put me on a bike to catch up to you. This is white privilege in a nutshell: what we've done in America is said, "Okay, Emmanuel, you're free to run." Meanwhile, we've acted as if it's been a fair race, when in all honesty, black people were held back for hundreds of years. And still are.

Lincoln's Emancipation Proclamation was the starting gun. All right now, black people, you're free, start running. Oh, one thing: I know we promised you "forty acres and a mule," but we're actually going to give that land back to the white people who started this war. Also, watch out for hurdles—here are laws to make it hard to vote, here are landowning practices to keep you poor and in debt, sharecropping for generations on the land you were promised. Then in the early 1900s, we say, "Yeah, we know we've created these Jim Crow laws to keep you segregated, but, black people—you keep right on running. Come on and catch up." Then in the late 1960s, we say, "Okay, black people, you can really go now, we've signed the Civil and Voting Rights Acts. Run harder and faster (we've seen how fast you can run) and catch us if you can." LBJ said it best: "You can't shackle and chain someone for hundreds of years, liberate them to compete freely with the rest and still justly believe that you've been fair."

You might be wondering, "Okay, so that's the history, but what about now? What about poor white people, how can they still be 'privileged'? What about rich and powerful black people? Still *un*-privileged?"

The short answer is: remember what I said about the race. It started more than four hundred years ago, and there are no redos. And white privilege is about the word *white*, not *rich*. It's having advantage built into your life. It's not saying your life hasn't been hard; it's saying your skin color hasn't contributed to the difficulty in your life.

Let's Rewind

WHILE THE TERM existed before she did, scholar Peggy McIntosh is credited with igniting a broad conversation around white privilege in her groundbreaking 1988 essay, "White Privilege: Unpacking the Invisible Knapsack." McIntosh defines white privilege as "an invisible package of unearned assets which I can count on cashing in each day, but about which I was 'meant' to remain oblivious. White privilege is like an invisible weightless knapsack of special provisions, maps, passports, codebooks, visas, clothes, tools and blank checks."

So just what is all this backpack junk? For many white people, white privilege is the power of feeling normal. It's the silent reinforcement of being able to walk into a store and see its main displays show products that cater to you. It's the ability to turn on the TV and see people who look like you represented in all walks of life. It's passing the corner office at work and seeing someone who could have been you once upon a time, and maybe finding mentors who "see themselves in you." It's never wondering whether the name on your résumé is "too white"; it's talking the way your local news anchor talks, the way the authorities say is "standard" or "proper." It's something as simple as having a Band-Aid, or a foundation color, match your skin. It's never having been the one the Photos app thinks is a gorilla.

The way I see this, it's kind of like being on the hometown team everywhere you go. You know the fans are going to be cheering for you and that most everyone in the stands wants you to win. Everyone is ready to give you advice. Everyone likes your uniform, and you got the new helmet, pads, cleats—all the equipment you need to succeed. You're all set up to win.

Meanwhile, the road team has the secondhand pick of everything.

Another part of white privilege is the omnipresent benefit of the doubt. It's the safety of moving through the world without being profiled, without worrying that the police might harass you or worse just because of your skin. It's the gift of not having your complexion be the reason someone mistrusts you financially, doesn't show you the nice apartment, doesn't give you the loan. It's never worrying that one riot, one gang, one criminal, one *anything* might mean more prejudice against you, too.

If you're accused of a crime, it's the presumption of innocence until proven guilty, the presumption of innocence sometimes even when proven guilty. It's having a picture of your smiling high school graduation photo if ever the news reports that you are connected to a serious crime. To get back to the hypothetical game, it's like having the refs on your side. If there's a call that could go one way or another, you're pretty sure it's going to go your way. They might even bend the rules for you.

Okay, I'll stall the sports analogy. But you get what I'm saying. We'll get a lot further into how this plays out in law enforcement, but let me give you one of the most infamous cases of "benefit of the doubt" in history. In 1955, Carolyn Bryant Donham claimed that a fourteen-year-old black boy, Emmett Till, grabbed her, menaced her, and made a sexually crude remark. Her white community believed her, and Till was captured, beaten beyond recognition, shot in the head, tied by barbed wire to a cotton gin, and thrown into Mississippi's Tallahatchie River.

None of it was true. Donham lied, pure and simple. If she hadn't, Till might be a happy grandfather right now; instead, he's a symbol of white privilege weaponized. In what's beyond a historical footnote, an all-white jury acquitted those two white men in September 1955. In a public interview just months later, they admitted that they did it, knowing they couldn't be tried again because of double jeopardy. In what's waaaaay beyond a footnote, Donham recanted her story in 2017.

Now imagine knowing all this and walking through the world as me. Imagine clocking every time a white woman crosses the sidewalk or ends up on the elevator with you; imagine having to avert your gaze so you don't make a white person uncomfortable, or changing your stride in front of police. Imagine always having to be on guard to gauge whether you are being perceived as a threat or are in some way playing into some white person's negative image or idea of you. Look, I've played a lot of sports and, let me tell you, there is no training that has equaled the exhaustion of having to live life this way all the time, not four quarters of a game but the sixteen hours or so of every day of my waking life.

To address the rich-versus-poor question. Yes, there are poor white people, and yes, there are rich black people. But let's scope out—white privilege is economic, too. The average net worth of a typical white family in 2016 was $171,000, a figure nearly ten times greater than that of a black family, at $17,150. TEN. TIMES. GREATER. Put another way, black people own about one-tenth of the wealth of white people in this country, adjusted for population. And check this: the wealth gap persists regardless of a household's education, marital status, age, or income.

Now you tell me if the race is fair.

Let's Get Uncomfortable

LET ME SAY right here that I know I have my own privilege. I'm a man, for one, and we've been oppressing women since the earliest civilizations. I'm also ablebodied. I'm also from a solidly middle-class family. I played professional football. All of those things grant me privilege in the world. I'm not saying that a black person can't have privilege or that a white person hasn't earned anything in their life. What I'm saying is that a white person's skin color isn't the thing contributing to holding them back, and that for all black people, their skin color contributes to what's hard about their lives no matter what other privileges they might enjoy.

White privilege is a hard conversation because we all want to believe in the American dream. We want to believe that America is both a democracy and a meritocracy, where all of our lives are the result of our own hard work and ambitions. I believed exactly that, all the way until I was getting my master's degree and took a class called Social Determinants of Health. Only then did I realize that not only do some people not start from zero, a lot of black people start in the negatives. And that's just not fair.

I'm guessing if you're white and have been reading and even halfway paying attention up to this point, then you realize that the excuse of ignorance is becoming less viable by the page. My friends, don't panic. That's a good thing.

Talk It, Walk It

IS IT POSSIBLE for white privilege to be eliminated? To even out the four-hundred-year head start?

This country won't change in a significant way until the majority of white Americans acknowledge and address their white privilege. Let's practice. You, dear reader, have white privilege. It's okay. Just sit with it for a minute: embrace it. Your discomfort means that the medicine is doing its job. Now, next time someone calls you on it, don't disengage from the moment or, as we used to say, don't take your ball and go home. Instead, focus on what a person of color might be feeling. Learn when is the time to listen intently, when is the time to be a megaphone for the voices of black people, and when is the time to step in and speak up. If white people are the problem, white people must also be part of the solution. I believe that.

One more thing to leave you with. I had a conversation with Carl Lentz, lead pastor of Hillsong Church NYC (my bro is one of the hippest pastors around), about white privilege, and he shared a conversation he'd had with another white man. "'It's just not real,'" Carl quoted the man as saying.

"Okay," Carl said. "Let's just say it's not real. Let's just say I'm wrong about white privilege—but I believe in it. It means I will have lived my whole life looking out for other people. Making sure everybody else gets the first shot and I get the second. Make sure people who are not in the mix get in it." If he found out he was wrong after all that, he'd still have a life of good deeds to show for it.

On the other hand, Carl told the man, "If *you* find out that you were wrong at the end of your life, that white privilege was real and you didn't acknowledge it, it means that you were stepping on the necks of others your whole life. Even if I'm wrong, my wrong is better than your wrong. What do you have to lose?"

To all of my readers who are wavering on whether white privilege is real, I pose the same question Lentz posed to the skeptical white man. What do you have to lose by believing in it?

"If there is a hairstyle or style in general that someone thinks is beautiful and wants to try out, but it is mainly seen in black women/ men, when is it not cultural appropriation?" —Kerri

4.

CITE YOUR SOURCES OR DROP THE CLASS

Cultural Appropriation

What would America be like if we loved
black people as much as we love black
culture?

—AMANDLA STENBERG

A couple of months ago, Kim Kardashian posted videos of herself on Instagram wearing a headful of white-beaded braids. Some of her followers weren't impressed:

"You are not black."

"Girl if u don't stop with the braids."

"How does she keep getting away with it?"

Kim K had tried to "get away with it" before, when in a now-infamous Snapchat video she was seen rolling in a car, talking about how much she loved her freshly twisted "Bo Derek braids." The internet jumped all over the post, pointing out that her hair was actually not in "Bo Derek" braids but Fulani braids, patterned after the styles of the Fulani people of West Africa. (If you're too young for Bo Derek, look her up—suffice it to say she's not from West Africa.) Black Twitter was hot because not only did Kim appropriate a black hairstyle, she gave a white woman credit for it. Talk about salting a wound.

Or let me put it to you like this. When I was in college, my professors warned us about plagiarism: using someone else's words or ideas without attributing them. Plagiarism was not only considered wrong, it was an offense that got you in serious trouble, up to getting kicked out of school. While it might be true that imitation is the highest form of flattery, plagiarism isn't flattery—it's stealing. It's doing none of the work yourself and taking as much of the credit as the world will give you. It's not knowing or caring what kind of struggle went into someone else's creation but using it to get yourself a passing grade—or a few thousand Instagram likes.

Borrowing influences from black culture is not an issue in and of itself. The problem becomes when you borrow from a culture without citing the sources and/ or knowing the history. As long as you do both of those things, you should be fine in most cases. (Key word—*most*.)

So just when does something move from homage, creative influence, or flattery into the bad kind of copycatting—the realm of cultural appropriation? When should white people be called out for engaging with cultures that aren't theirs—and when is a braid just a braid?

Let's Rewind

IN THE 1830S, a white actor named Thomas "Daddy" Rice got a bright idea. After witnessing a formerly enslaved person singing a song called "Jump Jim Crow," he created the character that would make him famous: a fictional caricature of a clumsy, dimwitted enslaved person named Jim Crow. Rice would don blackface, smearing on tar-like makeup and drawing exaggerated red lips, and perform a comedic "minstrel show" mocking black people. His show was a huge hit among white audiences all over America and as far as Great Britain. It wasn't long before other white minstrels were making a mockery of black people and culture and being celebrated for it.

You probably know where Jim Crow went from there. That's right: even the *name* for the laws that kept the South segregated until the 1960s was a cruel hundred-year-old joke at the expense of black people. You know where blackface went from there, too, because we're still talking about it. The list of white public figures with blackface scandals is ever growing, and although we could spend time listing all the surprise offenders, the more important point is that *this* is why you always need to know the history before you borrow from black culture. You might think you're being a fan by repping Beyoncé's look for Halloween, but what your deep-bronzed face evokes for a lot of black folks is the spirit of Thomas Rice and his minstrel shows. (And just so we're clear, blackface is one of those cases where knowing the history still doesn't make it okay.)

The exchange of ideas, styles, and traditions is one of the tenets of a modern multicultural society. It's a part of how we grow, learn, advance. But cultural appropriation is something else. Cultural appropriation happens when members of a dominant group—in the United States, white people—take elements from the culture of a people who are disempowered. It's problematic for a number of reasons. For one, it trivializes historic oppression. It also lets people show love for a culture while still remaining prejudiced toward the people of the culture and lets privileged people profit from the labor of oppressed people. On top of that, it can perpetuate racist stereotypes.

Let's dig into some more examples. Think of Little Richard inventing rock and roll and Elvis being considered the "king" of it. Think of jazz developing in the black community and Kenny G being maybe the most famous contemporary jazz artist. Think of hip-hop's birth in the Bronx, an art form meant to draw attention to the struggle of people of color, and years later the highest selling rap artist of all time being Eminem. Still not convinced of the ubiquity of cultural appropriation? Let me point to Blake Lively flaunting her curves at Cannes one year with the caption, "L.A. face with an Oakland booty." Try the Washington Redskins' culturally insensitive mascot (shout-out to the team for changing their name to the Washington Football Team in 2020). Try the Cleveland Indians' culturally insensitive mascot (shout-out to the team for considering a change—at least they got rid of Chief Wahoo). Sports is a biggie, but major fashion houses have been offenders, too. See Gucci selling a head scarf called the Indy Full Turban. See Prada selling a key chain with a blackface caricature. See a Burberry model strutting down the runway sporting a noose. Yes, a noose! And on and on.

Let's Get Uncomfortable

CULTURAL APPROPRIATION IS always an uncomfortable conversation. Think of how long black people have been demeaned in America. Think of how long their speech, their bodies, their skin color, their culture has been seen as lesser than. Now imagine how hurtful it would be to have those same characteristics taken on by white people and celebrated as their own. (Not to pick on Kim K, but homegirl's been credited with starting the current "booty boom," too—something for which black women were so long denigrated and which suddenly belongs to everyone now that it's popular.) Conversations must be had about what is and isn't cultural appropriation, about the history of what is being appropriated, about how it makes people who have long been disenfranchised feel.

Look, I get what y'all are coming for—call me biased, but black people do have a lot of the coolest music, the best looks, the baddest athletes. Taking the brag down a notch, black people have brilliant, creative people in every realm of American life, who have been doing brilliant, creative work for generations, because of course we do. The goal of sounding the alarm about cultural appropriation is not to stop anyone, white people included, from celebrating black culture. The key is to celebrate it *as black culture*—not to take it as your own. The discomfort comes in the gray areas, I know. Just trust me that asking more questions, doing more homework, is better than maybe plagiarizing any day.

Talk It, Walk It

IF YOU'RE INTERESTED in aspects of black culture, in braids or another hairstyle, in wearing ethnic fashion, in listening to black music or reading literature by people of color or watching movies grounded in another culture, you should do your homework. Find out about the genesis of the culture you want to engage with. If you want to wear braids, fine. But research where they came from. Be able to talk about it. It will keep you from attributing a style to Bo Derek—a woman who's only sixty-three years old—that has been around for hundreds if not thousands of years. I'm not saying everybody needs to become a historian, but if you're unsure about whether to engage with an aspect of black culture, talk about it with people who are informed. Yes, it might be uncomfortable, but there's a strong chance it will also be enlightening.

A few notes for the road. Blackface is never okay, not for any reason. Steer clear of adopting any ethnic stereotype: we could go through specifics all day, but basically if whatever vibe you're going for relies on evoking a race that is not your own, don't. And please think *extra* hard about adapting sacred cultural artifacts. No wampum belts or Sikh turbans, please. Finally, make a point to engage with cultures on more than an aesthetic level. If the first goal here is to stop being ignorant, the second goal is just to learn more about one another. And that can be a lot of fun.

"I have unfortunately encountered many black people who seem hell-bent on hanging the history of slavery and racism and inequality around every single white person's neck. Who are unwilling to give grace if we ask questions to try and understand how we can be better. They are angry and I'm not saying it isn't justified—anger is a form of grief and it's allowed to a degree within the law. But if we all genuinely want to move forward, this is an obvious problem." —Amy

5.

THE MYTHICAL ME

Angry Black Men

To be a Negro in this country and to be
relatively conscious is to be in a rage almost
all the time.

—JAMES BALDWIN

In Laurie Cassidy's article "The Myth of the Dangerous Black Man," she invites her reader into a thought experiment. Imagine yourself walking down a dark city street at night, she writes, and encountering a trio of young black men. She goes on:

> What do you do as these young black men approach? How do you feel as they walk by on the sidewalk? What do you do as they pass you? . . . How do you see these three young men in dress, appearance, and demeanor? If you are a white person reading these lines, ask yourself if you would feel apprehensive or frightened? Do you make eye contact and say

"hello," or do you keep your eyes focused on the ground? Do you imagine that they are carrying weapons? Are you afraid that they might mug you? And do you feel guilty that you even feel this way? After seeing these young men do you feel more vulnerable to physical harm and are you more alert to your surroundings?

Cassidy, who identifies herself as a middle-aged white woman, admits that she'd be "apprehensive" in the above scenario. But she also critiques her reaction, admitting that her response would not be based on actual experience with young black men, rather on ideas she's learned about them. While Cassidy uses the word *learned*, I'd take it a step further and call those ideas *indoctrination*. This is what happens when implicit biases are absorbed and, instead of being educated away, are reinforced. They turn into stereotypes that make it harder for every black person to live a life free of racism. And none of these stereotypes is more pervasive, and more harmful, than the myth of the Angry Black Man.

Have you heard of it? Or can you remember what you did in a situation like the one Cassidy describes? How would you answer the same questions that she posed to herself?

Let's Rewind

THE ANGRY BLACK Man is a two-parter—so bear with me, we have history to dig into here. The current implication is someone who recognizes racism and discrimination everywhere he looks, even when he's not a victim. One could also call the Angry Black Man a woke black man (see the James Baldwin quote that begins this chapter). But there's always a disparaging sense to it: like, here comes the Debbie Downer of Racism, the man who cried racist wolf.

This is an unfair characterization, but to unpack why, we have to dig back to another Angry Black Man stereotype. This is the black man as overly aggressive, menacing, and physically threatening, especially to innocent white women. That stereotype has been prominent since at least 1915, when Hollywood produced its first blockbuster film, *The Birth of a Nation*. At one point in the film, a black man proposes marriage to a white woman, and she runs and jumps off a cliff because she thinks he will rape her. Think about all the history that made that a reaction the filmmakers knew their audience would applaud. Not only did the film inspire the second coming of the KKK, it was also shown in the White House and impressed President Woodrow Wilson so much that he commented, "It's like history written in lightning." Off-screen, this false narrative about black men and their relationship to white women has been passed down for generations. The murderous practice of lynchings, so white men claimed, often had at its heart the goal of protecting the chastity of white women.

As with many myths, the Angry Black Man has

some truth to it. Not the systematic assault on white women—the anger. In the time of slavery, black women were often sexually exploited by white men. (Read up on Thomas Jefferson and Sally Hemings.) Now, imagine you were a black man and the woman you'd claimed as your wife (legal marriages between slaves weren't allowed) was raped by your white master or overseer. Not only was she raped but she was impregnated and gave birth to the master's child, and there was nothing you could do about it. Try to imagine the kind of hurt and anger you'd feel if this happened to you once, twice; if it happened to your children; if you suspected it had and would go on for generations.

On the other hand, imagine that if you so much as looked sideways at a white woman, if you did nothing but were accused of violating her respect and/or chastity, you could be captured, beaten, and lynched by a posse of white men. And when it was all over, that there would be nothing your people could do lest they suffer the same fate as you. And no consequences for the white people who murdered you. If that were your reality, if that were the history of your forebears, how angry would you be? At what point would you get over that anger? How in the heck would you get over that anger?

LET'S BRING IT back. The upshot of these stereotypes has been to allow what I think of as an ongoing "weaponizing of whiteness." We've already seen an example of this, with the murder of fourteen-year-old Emmett Till. More recently, you may have met Karen.

She is Amy Cooper, who in early 2020 called the cops on a bird-watcher in Central Park because he wanted her to leash her illegally unleashed dog. When she dialed 911, she used three words that are almost a death sentence to black men: "There's a black man who's *threatening my life.*" That was a lie, and thank goodness the birder had the video receipts. She's also Jennifer Schulte, dubbed "Barbecue Becky," who called the police on two black men legally barbecuing in an Oakland park. "I'm really scared. Come quick," she said, code for "Do harm to these black men." And she is Alison Ettel, dubbed "Permit Patty," who called the police on an eight-year-old black girl selling water in San Francisco without a license. "I need to see your permit," she said.

Names aside, they're all Karen, the meme: an entitled white woman who throws tantrums, asks to speak to the manager, and sometimes calls for the cavalry against a supposed Angry Black Man. Karen is also the granddaughter of a much older figure, "Miss Ann." Miss Ann was the name enslaved black people gave to white mistresses who exerted power over them on plantations. That's right—not only is there a long history of white women using their whiteness as a tool of control, there's a long history of meme-ing it.

Lest white men catch a break here, have you ever heard of Black Wall Street? In 1921, a black teen named Dick Rowland entered an elevator in Tulsa, Oklahoma. Minutes later, the white woman working the elevator screamed, and Rowland fled. He was arrested the next day for assaulting her. A mob of angry white people showed up at the jail demanding the authorities release Rowland into their custody, while a posse of armed black people showed up to protect Rowland from what was a sure lynching. You can bet the black people who showed up to save Rowland were not ignorant of Miss Ann and the ways she'd been protected over time, nor ignorant of how black men had been demonized as angry and dangerous.

The conflict between those brave black people and the white Tulsans who wanted Rowland's life erupted into what's now known as the Tulsa Race Riot or Tulsa Massacre. Those angry white people burned an area of Tulsa known as Black Wall Street, which was the economic beacon you probably guessed it was, killing an estimated 300 people, destroying more than 1,200 homes, and burning down almost all other structures. (Meanwhile, Dick Rowland would be found not guilty: he had tripped and accidentally grabbed the elevator operator.)

Bring it back up to the present, and this is what makes a George Floyd possible, or a Trayvon Martin— any time someone has been seen as a threat because they've first been seen as black. There's a video that's shown up on my social media feeds a few times, one I first saw on activist Shaun King's Facebook feed. The video shows a white guy named Jerry who is resisting the arrest of two cops. Jerry wrestles with the two officers, manages to grab one of their batons, and beats one of them with it. Meanwhile, someone outside the frame can be heard saying, "Jerry, they're gonna hurt you . . . Jerry, don't do it." Jerry isn't hearing it, though. After huffing a moment, he proceeds to jump in the officers' car and drive off.

I invite you to pause here and think of all the times you've seen or read about police shooting a black man for little more than twitching. I invite you to read up on (or watch the video of, if you can stomach it) the death of Rayshard Brooks. Brooks was drunk but was the calmest, most respectful drunk I've ever seen. He was trying to de-escalate the conflict with an arresting officer. Then while he ran away with a Taser that no longer worked, Atlanta PD officer Garrett Rolfe shot him twice in the back.

Let's compare: Both Rayshard and Jerry resisted arrest. Only one of them beat the police with their own weapon, then stole their car and sped off. And only the other one died.

Let's Get Uncomfortable

LIKE I SAID, in many cases, the anger of the black man is justified, if not for an immediate offense, then for the long train of historic offenses. It's not white people's job to police the feelings of black people, but as fellow human beings, please grant black people the right to the full gamut of emotions regarding their wounds.

You've likely heard of Karen and recognized the name as a pejorative. And there's a good chance you've seen a version of an Angry Black Man in the media. The memes, the images, the art . . . they are all political. The uncomfortable conversation is, where do these stereotypes come from? Who do these stereotypes serve? In what ways, if any, have you perpetuated them? If you've found yourself upset by Karen becoming a meme, ask yourself if you're looking at her in the fullest historical and cultural context. Ask yourself if you're equally disturbed by the myth of the Angry Black Man and what's happened as a result of that myth.

In the opening of this chapter, I talked about Laurie Cassidy's article "The Myth of the Dangerous Black Man" and how she recognized that her feeling threatened by black men was unjustified. That's a good place for anyone to start.

Talk It, Walk It

YOU MAY BE wondering by now: Am I angry? This chapter may come across that way. But there's really no other way for me to speak this truth.

Sometimes I am angry. Just like you are.

What you can do right now is start paying attention to how many times white people weaponize their whiteness against black people and how many times the myth of the Angry Black Man leads to violence against one of them. If you are a white woman, please don't be a Karen. If you're a white man, please don't be a white man with a gun pointed at my brother.

I also invite you all to read social justice educator Robin DiAngelo's book *White Fragility* and also historian Ibram X. Kendi's *How to Be an Antiracist*. If you have children, try *Stamped: Racism, Antiracism, and You* by Ibram X. Kendi and Jason Reynolds, or Mahogany Browne's *Woke Baby*. We got to start the youngins out right.

I want to leave you with this: if you see a black man and he is angry, obviously don't assume he's angry because he's black, but also don't assume he's even angry at anything racism-related in that moment. Let people have emotions. See him as an individual.

"Why do I have to bleep myself when I'm singing in my car to a black-authored song? Why can't I quote the lyrics or even sing the music that black artists themselves sell in the public domain?" —Chris

6.

NOOOOOPE!

The N-Word

> I will fight every nigger in here.
>
> **—RILEY COOPER**

Let me preface this by saying I thought Riley Cooper was cool. He'd played receiver for the Florida Gators and won national championships with Tim Tebow. He was a country dude, but I always thought he was good people. The year this infamous incident happened—2013—Cooper and I were teammates on the Philadelphia Eagles. It all started at a Kenny Chesney concert (well, his feelings on race clearly started before that), where a purportedly drunk Cooper was upset that he wasn't being allowed backstage and said, "I'll jump over the fence and fight every nigger in here!" He said it with the hardest *ER*.

Not too long afterward, I was chilling after lunch in the Eagles training facility while a video of the incident spread around the building like wildfire. Some of my black teammates were ready to fight Cooper, saying they couldn't wait till they saw him again. Couldn't wait. Next thing we knew, though, our head coach had given Cooper a few days off of practice to "rethink his actions"—as if taking time off during training camp, the most grueling part of an NFL season, was some kind of punishment! I couldn't believe it. Neither could my teammates, and those days off did little to heal the rift between them and Cooper. After that, any time he got the ball during our inter-squad practices, dudes were coming for his head.

Four months after the Cooper controversy, a white Miami Dolphins lineman called one of his black teammates a "half nigger" in a voice mail. The following season, the NFL tried to ban the word, establishing a rule that gave their referees the leeway to issue a fifteen-yard penalty for a first offense and an ejection for the second. Two seasons later, Colin Kaepernick started kneeling to protest the brutalizing and killing of black people at the hands of police. Please know all these things are interrelated.

Let's just get the basics out of the way right now: No. You can't use "nigga," or any other variation. There will never be any circumstances under which a white person should use the word *nigger*. Period.

Imagine the worst insult you've ever received. Now imagine that when you heard those words, what you also heard was that you're second-class forever. That you don't deserve any of this American dream. Imagine what you heard was: *You're an animal.* Imagine you heard, *You're stupid. You're a slave. My people owned your people, and you were better off when they did.* Imagine that you heard, *You won't amount to anything, boy. And the nothing you get is exactly what you deserve.* If you can picture one word communicating all of that, then you'll have some sense of what hearing the N-word does to me and any other black person in America.

I invite you to take a moment and look at this chapter's epigraph again. Sit with the word. I hope it shocked you a little when you read it; it was meant to.

Let's Rewind

WE CAN TRACE the word all the way back to the Latin *niger*, which simply meant "black." This became *Negro* in the Americas when colonist John Rolfe (the guy who married Pocahontas!) wrote a letter to a British official describing the arrival of "20 and odd Negroes" in the Jamestown colony of Virginia. In 1775, the first derogatory usage of the term *nigger* shows up—and boy, did that catch on. By the 1800s, the term had entered the American lexicon, and from the eighteenth century on, usage of the word and its attendant imagery exploded, showing up on cigarette boxes, on food packaging, on TV and movie screens, in books, in music, in lily-white neighborhoods. Remember this counting game: "Eeny, meeny, miny, moe, catch a tiger by his toe. If he hollers let him go"? Well, there was a time when that toe didn't belong to a tiger. All with the express purpose of demeaning black people.

The word fell out of favor and widespread usage by black people during the time of the civil rights movement, thanks in no small part to thinkers like James Baldwin, who were reimagining just who was a nigger: "We have invented the nigger. I didn't invent him. White people invented him," Baldwin said. "I've known and I've always known . . . that I'm not a nigger." Yet the term got picked up again as hip-hop became a cultural juggernaut in the late 1980s. Years before Ice Cube was a family-friendly addition to movies like *Are We There Yet?* or *Ride Along*, he was a scowling member of the late 1980s Compton rap group named N.W.A: Niggaz Wit Attitudes. From the height of the group's early 1990s popularity till now, the word *nigga* has been a staple in rap lyrics.

Niger, nigger, nigga. The last version is the form of the word that black people have used to seize some of the power of the word, to turn something that was meant to harm into something that might just have the potential to heal. *Nigga* is a term of endearment between some black people—the softening of the hard *ER* is key, as is the fact that it's reserved for intimate, black-to-black exchanges. It's a way for black people to commune, to create a space that's only for us. It is not, like any of the other forms of the word, a word that is available to white people.

This usage is not without its detractors. Maya Angelou once said, "The N-word was created to divest people of their humanity. When I see a bottle [and] it says 'P-O-I-S-O-N' then I know [what it is]. The bottle is nothing, but the content is poison. If I pour that content into Bavarian crystal, it is still poison." This was Angelou's response to those black people, like Ice Cube, who had reappropriated and assimilated the word. She appears to have thought that there was no softening or sanitizing or transmuting it, even for her own people.

In a move aligned with Angelou's thinking, the NAACP held a funeral for the word in Detroit. That 2007 ceremony included two Percheron horses, a pine box adorned with a bouquet of fake black roses and a black ribbon, and white-gloved pallbearers. The ceremony was presided over by then Detroit mayor Kwame Kilpatrick (a man who, though he may have meant well, proved himself of questionable character). "Today we're not just burying the N-word, we're taking it out of our spirit," said Kilpatrick. "We gather, burying all the things that go with the N-word."

Kilpatrick and the NAACP didn't succeed in banishing/burying the N-word. Four hundred years later, it's still the most infamous word in American culture.

And many black people still argue that using *nigga* or *niggah* or other derivations is, rather than poison, a way to empty the word of some of its original malice. What's more popular in American culture than hip-hop, where *nigga* has been very much alive and well since the days of N.W.A? Kendrick Lamar's hit "Alright" begins, "All my life I had to fight, nigga," and its chorus features, "Nigga, we gon' be alright." A few years later, Jay-Z released "The Story of O.J." off his *4:44* album, a song whose chorus includes, "Light nigga, dark nigga . . . Rich nigga, poor nigga . . . Still nigga, still nigga."

If black people do or don't say it, that's up to black people. Either way, unfortunately, there will always be white people, white men especially, who feel entitled enough to use the word. White entertainers sometimes think it can be made into a joke: like when Seinfeld actor Michael Richards used it repeatedly in a stand-up routine. Like when Louis C.K. used it in a conversation with Chris Rock. Like when a young Justin Bieber sang, "One less lonely nigger," captured on TMZ. Friends, it's not funny.

Let's Get Uncomfortable

CHRIS ROCK USED to have a part in one of his routines when he'd joke about the one instance when white people could use the word *nigger*. It went something like this:

"I'm going tell you the one instance when white

people can say nigger," he'd say, then would joke that white people were pumping their fist like, "This is what I paid for. It's a fucking great night now."

"The one time when white people can say *nigger*. Here it goes. Listen closely, because I may never say this shit again." He'd pause, that perfect long comedian's pause.

"Okay, if it's Christmas Eve. And it's between 4:30 and 4:49 in the morning. If you're white and you're on your way to Toys-R-Us to get your kids the last Transformer doll. And right before you walk into Toys-R-Us some black person runs up beside you. Smashes you in the head with a brick, knocks you to the ground. Stomps you in the face . . . river-dances on your head, takes your money, pisses on you, and runs away. If you're white, at that moment, you can say, 'SOMEBODY STOP THAT NIGGER.'"

And the crowd erupts.

Well, the crowd used to erupt way too loud for Rock, so much so that he decided to stop telling the joke. And I'm glad he did.

There is no conversation that excuses a white person using the word *nigger*. There's too much pain in that word coming from a white mouth. However, I will also say that if you're ever inclined to use it, you can and should investigate where that inclination or compulsion comes from. That's the difficult conversation—not *if* you should or shouldn't say it but *why* you could want to say it at all. If the word *nigger* is in your heart or on your tongue, please, please try to figure out why.

Talk It, Walk It

DURING HIS SCANDAL, Riley Cooper made an apology to us teammates in a private meeting. To tell the truth, I don't remember it, except to say that it seemed half-hearted. He also made a public apology over Twitter, from which the group he had actually targeted, *black people*, was notably absent:

"July 31 2013: I am so ashamed and disgusted with myself. I want to apologize. I have been offensive. I have apologized to my coach, Jeffrey Lurie, and Howie Roseman and to my teammates. I owe an apology to the fans and to this community. I am so ashamed, but there are no excuses. What I did Was wrong and I will accept the consequences." What consequences, you ask? Far as I could tell, part of Cooper's "consequences" was being rewarded with a five-year, $25-million extension. To be fair, he had what lots of people called a breakout season—but his reward seemed like the N-word and white privilege all bundled up into one huge billboard announcing the NFL's stance on racism.

Let's hope you won't need to make any private or public apologies for using the N-word. Instead, read Emerson professor Jabari Asim's book, *The N Word: Who Can Say It, Who Shouldn't, and Why*. Also, check out writer David Bradley's essay "Eulogy for

Nigger." As always, try to reflect critically on how you use language and the extent to which your language reflects your innermost thoughts and feelings. If you can't help yourself, I suggest you stop rapping along to the music.

Part II

US AND

THEM

"What systems are racist that need to be changed now? I have heard arguments about things related to housing and schools not being as well funded, which both seem to be more economic issues than race issues. I can see how in the past the now-grandparent generation may have suffered from racism under redlining and other practices that are now illegal. I also see how that can have lingering effects. However, I see those racist issues as having been dealt with." —Brianne

7.

THE HOUSE ALWAYS WINS

Systemic Racism

That dream of a land in which life should
be better and richer and fuller for everyone,
with opportunity for each according to
ability or achievement.

—JAMES TRUSLOW ADAMS, *THE EPIC OF AMERICA*, 1931,
COINING THE TERM *AMERICAN DREAM*

Months ago, I visited a white friend who'd just moved into a new house in Austin, Texas. It was a super-nice place: four bedrooms, huge space. I could tell how proud he was as he showed me around. Then, in the midst of the tour, he says, "Bro, check out these windows. They came with these plantation shutters."

It was like the record scratched on the happy soundtrack of the tour. I cringed. Good friend that he was, he saw my reaction and apologized. But the whole rest of the tour, and the rest of the day, I was thinking: *Why in the heck do we still have things called* plantation shutters? *And why are white guys buying homes where a real estate agent points out plantation shutters as a selling point? I mean . . . how could anyone hear of plantation shutters and not think of slavery?* Plantation shutters are a reminder of the worst thing America has ever done, and apparently they're still a plus on Zillow.

The signs aren't so overt everywhere, but don't ever let anyone convince you that we are in a "post-racial America." This term got thrown around a lot during the years 2008–2016—with a black president, how could America possibly still be racist? You don't hear the phrase so much anymore. But let me be clear: we will never achieve a post-racial America as long as the gears of systemic racism continue to churn. And believe me when I tell you, they are still churning, churning, churning away.

In 1931, historian James Truslow Adams coined the term *American dream*, seen in the opening epigraph. I'm sure we can all agree that an America built on "opportunity for each according to ability or achievement" sounds like a pretty great place to live. But it's a place that America has never been—especially for black people. We've already seen how the dream gets deferred on the individual level, in the everyday interactions between black and white

Americans: through implicit bias, white privilege, and cultural appropriation; through harmful stereotypes and punitive language.

Those everyday traces are the fingerprints of an even bigger, more deeply entrenched reality. (Here's your warning to strap in—this section of the book is gonna be a bumpy ride.) If you want to know the major reason America hasn't lived up to the stated ideals of its Founding Fathers, and of Mr. James Truslow Adams, it's due to a little thing called *systemic* (or *structural* or *institutional*) *racism*.

I'll be the first to admit that *systemic racism* sounds like a conspiracy. But guess what: if there is anything in America that fits the definition of a national conspiracy, it's systemic racism. Racism is a form of oppression, a.k.a. those with more power putting their thumbs on those with less power. And oppression is as old as civilization. Search as far back as you like: as soon as groups of people start creating rules for themselves, as soon as they start divvying up power, customs, a government—somebody is going to get oppressed. Sooner or later, there will be systems in place to ensure that some people fare better than others. In America, like many other countries founded on colonialism (even before we get to slavery!), the rule makers are white, and those faring worse are black and brown people.

Spoiler alert: a lot of those systems are still chugging along.

William Faulkner once wrote, "The past is never dead. It's not even past." Think about my friend's plantation shutters: the history of slavery literally hanging in plain sight. Think about Mississippi waiting until July of 2020 to remove *the literal Confederate flag* from its state flag. An evil, oppressive past is right here with us. And it's not hiding in plain sight. It's raising its arms and saying, "LOOK!"

Let's Rewind

IT'S TOUGH TO talk about systemic racism without sounding like a professor, so cut me a little slack for a couple of paragraphs. For starters, a definition: *systemic racism* is the legitimizing of every dynamic—historic, cultural, political, economic, institutional, and person-to-person—that gives advantages to white people, while at the same time producing a whole host of terrible effects for black people and other people of color. Those effects show up as inequalities in power, opportunities, laws, and every other metric of how individuals and groups are treated. Which is to say: systemic racism is making the unequal treatment of people of color the national norm.

I could spend the rest of this book detailing different parts of structural racism, but for now I'll take on a few major areas: housing, schooling, and criminal justice. The racism ingrained in each of these areas of life perpetuates a vicious cycle in which certain groups, including black folks, are held down, while other groups—namely, white folks—are elevated.

IF YOU'LL RECALL from the chapter on white privilege, black families have just one-tenth the wealth of white families. A big reason for that is real estate. One of the most common ways to build wealth is homeownership, and for decades there have been structural barriers in place to keep black people from reaping its benefits. Back in 1934, a dude named Homer Hoyt, then the chief economist of the Federal Housing Administration (FHA), wrote a report to help his agency standardize home-ownership loans in which he ranked various nationalities by order of "desirability." The most desired on the list were Anglo-Saxons and northern Europeans (this whole white-race business was still coming together), and at the bottom of the list were Mexicans and Negroes.

The FHA took this ranking and ran. They mapped out cities, dividing them into which neighborhoods were riskier to lend money, with no variable more important than race. Neighborhoods where the Protestant Anglos lived were marked in green, and, with other colors representing other groups in between, the neighborhoods where black people and Mexicans lived were marked in red. This is where we get the term *redlining*, which forced scores of black people into doing business with predatory lenders on homes in neighborhoods that were deemed undesirable and therefore less valuable than green—or rather white—neighborhoods.

Hoyt's thinking got codified across a bunch of real-estate practices, from biased homeowners' associations to hair-trigger evictions. And while redlining was outlawed in 1968 with the Fair Housing Act, it's still in practice in plenty of ways today, shaping what neighborhoods look like all over America. According to a 2016 Pew Research Center study, only 43 percent of black households are homeowners, contrasted with nearly 72 percent of white households. Add to that stat the fact that homeownership is the most common way to build generational wealth, and you can begin to see how white families pass down advantages to their children, while black families aren't able to set up their kids for the future. And the cycle continues.

Our public school system is just as flawed, and for related reasons. In most states, school funding breaks down like this: state taxes (45 percent), local taxes (45 percent), and federal taxes (10 percent). While states sometimes subsidize funding shortfalls, it's not usually enough to level the playing field. If the homes in a school's neighborhood are worth less than the homes of schools in other neighborhoods, then those owners pay less taxes. If there are fewer businesses in the particular neighborhood, there will also be much less tax revenue. So schools in poor neighborhoods are forced to do more with less. Not only that, the American educational system is de facto almost as segregated as it was during Jim Crow, because of those redlined neighborhoods, the defeat of busing programs, and lobbyists for local school districting—often simply (white) parents who want to make sure their good schools stay good. It all adds up to a system described by Pulitzer Prize–winning journalist Nikole Hannah-Jones as "separate and unequal."

And that's just the numbers. We also have to look at the history of the black community's relationship to schooling in this country. We must never lose sight of the truth that when black people were enslaved, they were forbidden to read and write, that their white owners did everything they could think of to keep them illiterate, undereducated, ignorant. Imagine what kind of effect that had on those enslaved people, and on their children, and their children. Here's a little more perspective. Founded in 1636, Harvard is the oldest institution of higher learning in America. The oldest historically black college and university (HBCU) is Cheyney University, founded in 1837. So, there's a two-hundred-year gap of higher education between white and black people.

Black people have had to face many hardships because of that gap, because of attending perennially underfunded schools, and because of white people for generations trying to indoctrinate them toward anti-intellectualism. Time after time, research has shown that gaps between black and white students begin early in childhood and only widen with age. The socioeconomic makeup of a school can play a larger role in achievement than the poverty of an individual student's family, and a poor education has a huge effect on later fortunes. You've likely heard how education is one of the greatest paths to upward mobility? Well, the Brookings Institution found in 2014 that black children are especially susceptible to downward mobility—nearly seven of ten black children born into middle-income families failed to maintain that income level as adults.

Then there is the possibility of jail or prison. Pick your stat: According to a 2012 Annie E. Casey Foundation study, a student failing to read at their grade level by the end of the third grade is four times less likely to graduate. According to a 2009 study by Northeastern University, high school dropouts are sixty-three times more likely to be incarcerated than college grads. You needn't be a statistician to see a correlation between schools and prisons, one that's now known as the *school-to-prison pipeline.*

Which brings me to the criminal justice system, yet another area where systemic racism is limiting the lives of countless black people and other people of color. In what's a ground-zero statistic, black people are much more likely to become involved in the criminal justice system, or, as those in the know say, more likely to become justice-involved than white people. At about 13 percent of the U.S. population, black people make up more than one-third of those in federal and state prisons. That overrepresentation is not an accident but the product of systemic racism. Black people are not any more criminal than anyone else (more on that in chapter 10), but they've been criminalized as much or more than any group in America.

Ironically, some say this started with a little adjustment to the U.S. Constitution called the Thirteenth Amendment. "Neither slavery not involuntary servitude, **except as a punishment for crime whereof the party shall have been duly convicted**, shall exist within the United States, or any place subject to their jurisdiction." Yeah, I bolded that clause for a reason. Plenty of scholars have linked that exception clause to the rise of what's now called *mass incarceration* or the *prison industrial complex*.

Around the time the amendment was passed, Southern white people were inventing Black Codes, laws that penalized black people for stuff like not showing proper respect or doing "malicious mischief," and punished those "crimes" as misdemeanors or felonies depending on how severe someone (almost always a white person) decided they were. Those vague laws coerced more black people into prison than ever before. It wasn't that black people had all of a sudden become criminals; it was that the laws began to criminalize black people. States were then able to put prisoners to work through "convict-leasing" deals that sent the imprisoned back to slave owners. While the

Thirteenth Amendment ended slavery on the surface, its loophole paved the way for returning many black people to slavery.

Prisons today don't have programs like that. They just have mandatory labor projects, sans a living wage, worked disproportionately by black people. Hmm.

Let's Get Uncomfortable

OKAY. DEEP BREATH. Systemic racism is hard to talk about because it seems so big, so pervasive. And it is. I've touched on a few of the places it rears, but the truth is that it pervades almost all areas of American life, even as it's hard to suss out just what role an individual white person plays in the system.

Let's address that last part head-on. White brothers and sisters, I hear you. None of this is your fault individually. And maybe you've traced your family tree back generations and found that neither your great-great-great-grandparents nor anyone else in your family owned slaves (prayer hands to that for sure). But on the other hand, can you trace your family tree as far back as it goes in America and claim that every single person on your family tree was a staunch abolitionist? That every single one of them denounced all aspects of their white privilege, called out racism wherever it arose, and that they were never the beneficiaries of white privilege in any of its forms? That's a much harder project. That might well be an impossible project.

I hope you see where I'm going with this. Remember what I said about white privilege, how you don't even have to do anything to have it work for you? Well, it's worked that way for as long as it's been around, which means you've likely spent your whole life enjoying the fruits of systemic racism and never having to directly engage with its fallout.

Luckily, you're here now to engage in the solution.

Talk It, Walk It

NO ONE CAN fight systemic racism alone. It's too big and in too many areas. On the flip side, that means there are a million ways to help.

As always, a good place to start is learning more. Visit the Urban Institute online (urban.org) for exemplary coverage of structural racism in cities. At your job, advocate for diversity. If your office doesn't have a diversity and inclusion team, push for one. Take political action whenever and wherever you can, voting for and holding accountable local and national officials, signing petitions, peacefully protesting when needed. Dismantling systemic racism is nothing short of dismantling white supremacy. It's going to take a herculean effort by all of us to tear it down.

"My question is about the term 'reverse racism.' It seems to me that it's an oxymoron. Isn't racism just racism—whether it's white people hating black people, black people hating Latinos, Latinos hating Asians, Asians hating white people, etc.? Hate based on skin color / nationality is just hate, and that's racism. Isn't the reverse of racism love?" —Tracy

8.

SHIFTING THE NARRATIVE

Reverse Racism

Those of us who know our whites know one thing above all else: whiteness defends itself. Against change, against progress, against hope, against black dignity, against black lives, against reason, against truth, against facts, against native claims, against its own laws and customs.

—TRESSIE MCMILLAN COTTOM

In my second year in the NFL, my first year with the Eagles, there was a six-four, three-hundred-plus-pound defensive lineman who just liked to bully me. Maybe he thought I didn't act tough enough, I don't know, but he was constantly on my head, telling other dudes not to hang out with me.

Really childish stuff. Finally, one day at practice, we were all in a huddle on the field, our helmets under our arms, all of us on one knee. The lineman was behind me, and I looked over my shoulder to see him pull another teammate to the side and lean in like he was going to whisper. Instead he said, loudly, "Don't stand next to Acho." I just shook my head. After the coach broke the huddle, I walked over to him and looked him straight in the face. "Bro," I said. "You are the worst teammate in the history of teammates." And I looked at him like I was ready to fight. All I was thinking was, *Let's fight and get it over with*.

We didn't end up fighting. But in that moment, it wasn't like I was being a reverse bully. It was just that I was finally standing up for myself.

NOW THAT WE'VE expanded our definition of racism to include the systems that feed it, I'd like to address another supposed flavor: reverse racism, a.k.a. the idea of black people (or anyone nonwhite) being racist against white people. I've had many people ask me if reverse racism exists. They often pair this with a second question: Is it even possible for black people to be racist?

The first thing to understand is that those are two very different questions. About the latter, I'll cite an answer Dr. Ibram X. Kendi gave during a CNN interview last year:

You have black people who believe that they can't be racist because they believe that black people don't have power and that's blatantly not true. Every single person on earth has the power to resist racist policies and power. We need to recognize that there are black people who resist it, and there are some who do not. And then you have black people, a limited number, who are in policy, making decisions to institute or defend policies that harm black people.

So there you have it. One of America's foremost experts on racism, dispelling the belief that black people can't be racist. But let me point out a couple of things. First, Dr. Kendi's claims concern black people being racist against other black people. Second, when he is talking about black people in a position to make policy either for or against racism, note the key phrase: *a limited number*.

When I say that reverse racism is a myth, what I mean is that, though individual black people can be prejudiced against white people, reverse racism by black people at large against white people at large just doesn't exist. It can't exist, because that's not how collective power works in this country.

What is reverse racism if it's not, well, real? It's a prime example of what scholar Alice McIntyre calls *white talk*: a.k.a. strategies white people use—consciously or not—to insulate themselves from their collective participation in racism. Another way into this idea is the term *white fragility*, popularized by sociologist Robin DiAngelo. When white people are put in situations that challenge their identity, "we withdraw, defend, cry, argue, minimize, ignore," explains DiAngelo. "And in other ways push back to regain our racial position and equilibrium." Put very simply—y'all get defensive. The feeling of defensiveness is white fragility, and the way you hit back, with accusations like reverse racism, is white talk.

I'll unpack more white talk below; some of it may be familiar to you. Stay with me. Keep your eyes and heart open. Unlike with that lineman, I'm not here to fight.

Let's Rewind

I REPEAT: THERE is no such thing as reverse racism. If you want to oppress someone, you're gonna need power over them as a group—and no group holds it over white people. There literally aren't enough black people with institutional authority over white people to facilitate systemic racism against them. On a purely numbers level, this would be tough; black celebrities may loom large in our society, but black people are still only 13.4 percent of the population (white people still make up 59.7 percent). While white people are predicted to be a statistical minority by 2045, black people are a long, long ways off, if not forever, from dominating the white world. Even if that became true, what are the chances that the majority of black people would focus on oppressing white people?

And yet, white folks argue in favor of reverse racism every day. Calling back to cultural appropriation, some people think it's reverse racism to get criticism for wearing dreadlocks or for renaming traditional African braids after a white woman. Others cry reverse racism for the forever ban on them using the N-word, especially if black people can use derogatory words for a white person (which I don't advocate) without the same backlash. But as I hope I've proven, these are straw-man arguments. They're what I mean by white talk.

One of the most common examples of white talk is calling Affirmative Action reverse racism. To explain why that's wrong, I want to take us back to 1961, almost a hundred years after the Civil War, when President John F. Kennedy signed Executive Order (EO) 10925, which instructed federal contractors to take "affirmative action to ensure that applicants are treated equally without regard to race, color, religion, sex, or national origin." That order was the nation's first instance of Affirmative Action. Since then, it's been implemented (and challenged) in a number of areas where systemic racism has persisted.

In a nutshell, Affirmative Action is an effort to redress the systemic inequalities caused by centuries of discrimination. To try to achieve measures of social equality, it gives preferential treatment to groups that have suffered those long-standing inequalities. Some people argue that it's unfair to now give black people preference and thereby treat white people unfairly. To that I say, what's fair? If you ask me, fairness can only occur between equal parties, and black people have never been treated as equals in America. As a matter of fact, unfairness doesn't even scratch the surface of how they've been treated.

"But *my* ancestors didn't own slaves," you may have heard. "Why should I be the one who doesn't get the job or the scholarship, who gets stuck on the waiting list?" Or "I grew up poorer than some of the black kids getting into universities on Affirmative Action; why shouldn't I get that leg up instead?" The thing is, one can never just judge racism on an individual level alone. It's also historic and systemic—remember, white people will always have that several-century head start.

Believe me, I sympathize with feeling like the work you put in isn't paying off, like you deserve something you didn't get, like odds are stacked against you. That said, there's a definite difference between a kind of unfairness that befalls you as the unintended effect of a policy that's rationally, empathetically trying to right years of wrongdoing and the kind of unfairness that is pursued as an end itself. Think about that: the unfairness black people have experienced has been the point of systemic racism, not the by-product of some other objective. What white people experience as unfairness as a result of Affirmative Action does not have as its aim being unfair to white people. And therein lies the main difference.

Another white-talk argument concerns the twenty-eight days of February, otherwise known as Black History Month. Why can't white people have White History Month? Let me take this from the top. Black history exists because of a black scholar named Dr. Carter G. Woodson, who in 1915 founded the Association for the Study of Negro Life and History (ASNLH). To promote awareness of black achievements, Dr. Woodson and his colleagues created the Negro History and Literature Week, soon renamed Negro Achievement Week. They marked the week in February because it was the birth month of both Frederick Douglass and Abraham Lincoln, men who played an integral role in shaping black history. Negro Achievement Week caught on like a stadium cheer: by the 1950s, it had expanded into a whole-month celebration, and in 1976 that shift was made official with the renaming of Negro Achievement Week into Black History Month. Every American president since the 1970s has endorsed that commemoration with an official proclamation.

There's no White History Month because we celebrate the accomplishments of white people Every. Single. Day. White people have always been esteemed in this country, have always been celebrated. Black people have had to push to celebrate themselves and their culture in public. (It's also why we often refer to each other as black kings and black queens. After a history of white society tearing black people down, it's about intentionally lifting each other up.) You ever read about the first black person to do so and so or hold such and such a job? I know I have. Here's the first black head football coach in the NFL. Here's the first black owner in the NFL. Here's the first black editor in chief of *Harper's Bazaar*. Here's the first black person to attend Harvard, the first black valedictorian at Princeton. Here's the first black woman to win a Pulitzer Prize. Now think of when you've ever heard about the first white person to do something significant. I can't remember one time reading, "Check it out, finally a white person's done this!" And you know why? Because white people have had a lock on significance since before this country was even a country. They've had a lock on opportunities, and they've had a lock on the institutions that report achievements, too. White people are celebrated every day for the great things they do. It's called the news. It's called the history books. It's called Mount Rushmore. It's called the White House. They're called Fortune 500 CEOs and college presidents and venture capitalists and Oscar winners.

All to say: No, it's not reverse racism to celebrate Black History Month. But it might be racist to call for a White History Month.

For similar reasons, it's at best insensitive to say

"All lives matter" when someone says that black lives matter. White lives have never been in danger from black lives to the degree that black lives have been endangered by white people and whiteness, and that's on an individual level and a systemic level. While some people say it to provoke conflict and others might do it for the sake of inclusivity, in either instance, it's insensitive and harmful. Novelist Jason Reynolds does a wonderful job of expanding on the reasons why:

> If you say, "No, all lives matter," what I would say is I believe that you believe all lives matter. But because I live the life that I live, I am certain that in this country, all lives [don't] matter. I know for a fact that, based on the numbers, my life hasn't mattered; that black women's lives definitely haven't mattered, that black trans people's lives haven't mattered, that black gay people's lives haven't mattered . . . that immigrants' lives don't matter, that Muslims' lives don't matter. The Indigenous people of this country's lives have never mattered. I mean, we could go on and on and on. So, when we say "all lives," are we talking about White lives? And if so, then let's just say that. 'Cause it's coded language.

When people proclaim that black lives matter, it's not about saying white lives don't matter. It is a given in this country that they do. What black people are really and truly saying is that black lives matter as well as white lives. Add to that list of false equivalents: black pride versus white pride, white privilege versus "black privilege." That last phrase is about as real as reverse racism.

Let's Get Uncomfortable

I CONSIDER MYSELF a sensible guy. And for me, a "fair" argument is one where there's probably some merit on both sides, where the moderate, rational person is looking for a path to compromise. So I get that somewhere there's a person used to hearing out arguments that says, "Well, if white people can be racist against black people, surely there must be *some* merit on the other side?" And here's my answer: don't fall for it! This simply isn't that kind of conversation. Remember it's a definitional thing, and "white" and "black" just aren't equal in this country, for all the systemic reasons we've said. I mean, come on, that would be like saying an attacker had a point if he tried to sue the victim.

Still, it's an uncomfortable conversation for a lot of reasons. For one, it makes all white people accountable. And I know it's hard to think you're paying for the wrongs of someone else. It's also hard because who doesn't want to be proud of what they've done, to be proud of what their ancestors have done? I feel you on that. Really, I do. But if you are going to be proud of the history of white people, you have to acknowledge the *whole* history of white people. And if we put all those great things in context, we must admit that they occurred in an America that rigged and denied opportunities to others, so that white people could thrive. And this is not to dismiss the talent, intelligence, drive, ingenuity, of all the great white people. Not to dismiss all those firsts from long ago and even now. But if we're going to talk about it, let's talk about all of it.

Talk It, Walk It

IT'S GOING TO take courageous, informed, empathetic, committed white people to challenge their racial peers who rely on white talk. If your goal is to fight racism, to help foster an America that isn't built on white privilege, then you'll have to do your part. Each and every one of you will have to do your part. Educate white friends and family on Black History Month. Talk to them about why a White History Month not only isn't needed but is actually another act of racism. Discuss with them how racism is on the hands of white people in general as well as white people in particular, how even though they might not believe themselves overtly racist, that they could be acting in a way that fosters racism or fails to discourage it.

To get more into the scholarship here, read Noel Ignatiev's *How the Irish Became White*, and if you're feeling ambitious, check out the rest of his books. I also suggest picking up *Racecraft: The Soul of Inequality in American Life* by Karen E. Fields and Barbara

J. Fields, and author Carol Anderson's *White Rage: The Unspoken Truth of Our Racial Divide*. Anderson is the head of African American studies at Emory University and delves into the feeling of anger white people have had over black equality and how that anger has manifested over the years. If you can make it to D.C., I encourage you to visit the wonderful National Museum of African American History and Culture, or if you can't, there may be a black (it's likely called African American) museum closer to you. If you're really excited about education, I suggest checking out the courses in the black studies (or African American lit) programs at your local colleges and universities.

While you're out there living your life every day, pay attention to how many times you hear something being touted as the first black X and how long it took for that thing to happen. Think about how weird it would sound to hear of the first white X to do something. If you're in room with a bunch of powerful people, take note of how many of them are white. Ask yourself: Would it have felt unusual if most of them were black? As you go through your days, pay attention to how often white is the default. Know that saying "All lives matter" means arguing that we're still not defaulting to white enough.

"What's the best way to make the most impactful contributions to dismantling the institutions and policies meant to keep POC at a disadvantage?" —Mike

9.

THE FIX

Who's Governing the Government

I'm not a Republican, nor a Democrat, nor an
American, and got sense enough to know
it. I'm one of the 22 million black victims of
the Democrats, one of the 22 million black
victims of the Republicans, and one of the
22 million black victims of Americanism.
And when I speak, I don't speak as a
Democrat or a Republican, nor an American.
I speak as a victim of America's so-called
democracy. You and I have never seen
democracy; all we've seen is hypocrisy.

—MALCOLM X, "THE BALLOT OR THE BULLET" (1964)

Good people, let me remind you that I was born
and raised in Dallas, Texas. During the 2016
election, I was living it up in my hometown and
looking for a polling station. Wouldn't you know

it, there was one at this church right by my crib. This was my first time voting in Texas (I had been in Cleveland for the last election, playing for the Browns). That is to say, I didn't know what to expect and was thinking that the poll station might have a crazy line. But when I pulled up to the church, there was nobody there except six or seven poll workers. I waltzed right inside, said hi to the nice white staffers, filled out my little ballot, submitted it, and waltzed my smiling self right back out. The whole thing took maybe three and a half minutes, hellos and good-byes included.

Now compare that to the 2018 midterms. At that time, I was living in Austin, Texas. My house was in a gentrifying area on the east side of town, and my closest polling station ended up being a Fiesta grocery store. I don't know if any of you have ever been to a Fiesta, but it's a popular chain in heavily Hispanic neighborhoods in Austin. During those 2018 primaries, I pulled up to Fiesta with the confidence of a dude who'd last voted in an affluent neighborhood, thinking I was going to walk my happy little butt into another polling station and zippety-do-dah right out. But when I turned the corner to park, I saw a line of at least two hundred people. *Man*, I thought, *what is this?* I walked inside to investigate and saw the line snaking around the store and back outside. I couldn't believe it. "Is this the line to vote," I asked, "or are they giving out free trips to the

Bahamas?" They were like, "No, no, no, this is the line to vote."

I was tempted to leave. I had a flight to catch; I didn't have two and a half hours to wait in line. But there was this sweet old black woman in front of me, and she said, "You'd better stay here, son. Remember all we went through to vote." I looked at her. I waited in that line.

Now picture this. While I was breezing through a polling station in 2016, not far away in Fort Worth, Texas, a woman named Crystal Mason walked to her local station to do what that old woman in Austin had reminded me to stay for. Mason, a mother of three, might not have voted had her mother not convinced her that it would set a good example for her kids. Mason trooped down to her local polling station, and to her surprise, her name wasn't registered on the voting rolls. Determined, she cast a provisional ballot, meant to be approved pending further checks. Mason was a formerly incarcerated person and as it turns out missed the fine print on her ballot that read, "I understand that it is a felony of the second-degree to vote in an election for which I know I am not eligible." Not only did Mason fail to see the words, she was also unaware of Texas's super-strict voting laws, the ones that actually made her ineligible to vote.

Three months after she voted, she was called into a Fort Worth courthouse, handcuffed, and charged with voter fraud. A year or so later, she was convicted of fraud and sentenced to the harshest penalty possible: five years in prison. It hardly seemed a fair judgment for the small oversight of a woman and mother of three who believed she was doing her civic duty.

Is America really a democracy? The short answer is no, it's technically a republic, or what some people term a *representative democracy*. Our laws are made by representatives we have chosen (in theory), who must comply with a constitution that was built (in theory) to protect the rights of the minority from the will of the majority. But the truest answer is that America has never been a republic for everyone who lives within its borders.

So we've got systemic racism, right? All these institutions like housing, schools, and prisons that keep disadvantaging people of color. You may have been asking yourself, If we have laws keeping these systems in place, why not just make new laws? Why not vote out racist people and practices? This chapter is about why not. There are tools, it turns out, by which (some of) those in power are still actively perpetuating racist systems and disenfranchising those who would change things—a.k.a. the voters. I call this whole situation *the Fix*. If we want an America that's not fundamentally racist, we must address the Fix, like, yesterday.

Let's Rewind

TWO OF THE most rigged parts of our democratic system are voting and jurors. Both these ways of participating in government have had more discrimination than we could cover in all four quarters and overtime of a tight game, so in the interest of space, I'll focus on the long history of voter suppression of black people, and the pernicious practice of rigging juries against black folks (and other POC).

You might've heard of a little thing called the electoral college. Yes, the confounding institution that awarded the 2016 election to Donald Trump and the 2000 election to George W. Bush, despite their opponents winning the popular vote in each case. You might remember from civics class that the electoral college was created because, during the Constitutional Convention, the Founding Fathers thought ordinary Americans wouldn't have enough information to make informed and intelligent voting decisions. While that may have been true, there was also another major factor being hashed out between those Northern and Southern delegates: what to do about five hundred thousand or so enslaved people. The result of that debate was what became known as the Three-Fifths Compromise.

Article 1, section 2 of the Constitution states: "Representatives and direct taxes shall be apportioned among the several states which may be included within this Union, according to their respective numbers, which shall be determined by adding to the whole number of free persons, including those bound to service for a term of years, and excluding Indians not taxed, three fifths of all other persons."

In layman's terms, the compromise counted each enslaved person as three-fifths of a human being for the purposes of taxes and representation. That agreement gave the Southern states more electoral votes than if they hadn't been counted at all, but fewer than if black people had been counted as a full person. And that political leverage paved the way for nine of the first twelve presidents being slave-owning Southerners. Keep in mind, those enslaved black people couldn't vote themselves, couldn't own property, nor take advantage of any of the other privileges available to white men. Not only was all their labor stolen from them, their bodies were symbolically used to grant their enslavers more power. If we're talking an electoral fix, the Three-Fifths Compromise is the ultimate.

A century on, as you know, the Thirteenth Amendment abolished slavery, which gutted the Three-Fifths Compromise. The Fourteenth Amendment then granted formerly enslaved people citizenship and gave black people supposed "equal protection under the law," while the Fifteenth Amendment declared, "The right of citizens of the United States to vote shall not be denied or abridged by the United States or by any State on account of race, color, or previous condition of servitude." So, game over? Of course not. It wasn't long before Southern states were inventing ways to skirt the Fourteenth and Fifteenth Amendments and keep black people from participating in American democracy.

No better place to start than with what were called *grandfather clauses*. Beginning with Louisiana, seven states between the 1890s and early 1900s passed statutes that allowed any person who'd been granted the right to vote before 1867 to continue voting without the need for a literacy test, owning property, or paying a poll tax. These were called *grandfather clauses* because white men (remember, women were decades from being granted the right to vote) were literally *grandfathered in*. Since most black people had been enslaved prior to 1867, they were denied the right to vote based on the clauses. They still had to be allowed to vote, legally, but states took care of the reality by requiring poll taxes (it's exactly what you think: paying to enter the polls), literacy tests (reading and writing had been forbidden under slavery), property ownership, and even constitutional quizzes (how does one pass one such test when he can't read or has never seen a source where the information is written?).

The Northern states weren't angels, by the way. For the purpose of "healing the union" after the Civil War, they basically let the South have their way and thereby squandered all the promise of Reconstruction. The way I see it, those Northern states were the devil's bargainers of the era: the fixers who, to ensure their own power, agreed that freedom didn't have to mean power for black people.

Voter suppression laws are not a bygone practice. They are in place right now, using new and refurbished tactics with the same old objective: to disenfranchise black people. Such as in Kansas, where a Republican secretary of state, Kris Kobach, championed a law that required proof of citizenship to vote on the pretense that noncitizens were voting illegally. That law failed because the U.S. Circuit Court of Appeals said that Kobach, a white man, "failed to prove the additional burden on voters was justified by actual evidence of fraud." During the time the law was in effect, thirty-one thousand applicants were prevented from voting, yet the appeals court noted that no more than thirty-nine noncitizens had managed to vote in the past nineteen years. Other states, including Arkansas, Pennsylvania, and North Carolina, have enacted voter ID laws using claims of voter ID fraud. This despite these ACLU stats: up to 25 percent of black citizens of voting age lack government-issued ID, compared to only 8 percent of white people.

Other strategies of voter suppression, a.k.a. the Fix, are state legislatures increasing or decreasing the number of polling stations in a given district, changing the times or days the stations are open, and even planting faulty machines in certain polling stations to slow them down. Another common tactic has been purging the registries of people who can vote. This is done by removing people from the voting registry who haven't voted for a certain number of years or haven't received a voting card mailed to their address.

This more often targets black people and poor people who have unstable housing.

And then there's gerrymandering. This is when a state redraws the boundary of a voting district to negate certain votes. Two ways to do this: One is "packing," where voters are clustered into a district predicted to be won by an oppositional party, so the extra votes are wasted on that party. The other is "cracking," when voters for a party are broken into multiple districts where the opposing candidate will win with a large majority, again wasting votes.

One more election Fix that's been getting attention: preventing people who've been convicted of a crime from voting. The length and kinds of restriction varies from state to state, from a lifetime ban up to people being disallowed to vote while incarcerated, and including restricting their ability to vote until they've completed parole or paid certain fees. Barring currently or formerly incarcerated people from voting doesn't only suppress black voters, it targets them disproportionately, since they are overrepresented in prisons and jails.

Sometimes these tactics fail, luckily. When the Wisconsin legislature insisted on curtailing voting by mail and held voting during the pandemic this year, the thinking was that their tactics would cause a much lower voter turnout of Democratic voters (more often tied to crowded inner-city polling stations and outside-the-home work schedules) and protect a conservative Wisconsin Supreme Court spot. Their plan backfired, instead inspiring a huge turnout that helped to unseat the conservative majority. And just a few months ago, a Florida federal judge ruled that a state law requiring felons to pay any outstanding fines before registering to vote is unconstitutional.

Too often, though, voter suppression succeeds.

WOULD IT SURPRISE you that another part of the Fix involves our courts and, in particular, our juries? Bryan Stevenson, a man who's dedicated his life to social justice (have you read the book or seen the movie *Just Mercy*?), describes American courts this way: "We have a system of justice that treats you better if you're rich and guilty than if you're poor and innocent." I would add to his adjective of *poor* the adjective of *black*.

Maybe no person knows this better than Timothy Foster, a man who in 1987 was convicted by an all-white jury in Georgia of murdering a white woman and sentenced to life in prison. Foster's case ended up before the U.S. Supreme Court, where it was discovered that Georgia had stricken black people from his pool of possible jurors, using a process known as *peremptory strikes*. The Supreme Court had ruled the selection of jurors by race to be unconstitutional just a year before Foster's trial, so peremptory strikes had become the loophole: a playbook of race-neutral reasons given to strike a black juror in the hope that one of those reasons will be found valid by the judge. News flash: one of those reasons is often found valid.

A little recap here. For almost a century, black people were not allowed to legally vote, even as their bodies (three-fifths each) were used to beef up the Southern vote. Then they get the legal right to vote, only to face all kinds of nefarious tactics to keep them from it. They then face a justice system not of their peers but white people (in 2017, 71 percent of U.S. district court judges were white), who send them to prison far more often than white people. Once freed, they face yet more obstacles to vote. Should they somehow vote by accident, they face more prison— and should they not vote, well, they have little means of changing the laws and those who make them.

A lose-lose situation, whichever way you look at it. That, brothers and sisters, is the nature of the Fix.

Let's Get Uncomfortable

BECAUSE OF VOTER suppression, there are fewer polling stations in places of lower socioeconomic status, particularly liberal places in Republican states. Back when I was in Dallas, my fancy neighborhood with the breezy voting experience was also a Republican area. But in Austin, I lived in a gentrifying area that is of a historically lower socioeconomic status. What I remember from that day was that several people left the line, and if I had to guess, I'd say some of them left because they couldn't afford to take off from work.

Voting privileges, juries: it's a difficult conversation for anyone who counts political ideologies as an important part of their identity, because you want to believe that your party is on the up-and-up. Our democracy is supposed to be fair and impartial, but the truth is that both Republicans and Democrats engage the Fix to some degree. You don't need to be a political scientist to see how unfair the political system has been to black people. We must continue to bring up these tough conversations, between one another, on our social media platforms, in our newspapers, and so on.

Crystal Mason waived her right to a jury. You have to wonder, why would a black woman in Texas waive her right to be tried by a jury of her peers? You have to wonder if it was because Mason did not believe she would get a fair trial by jury. You might wonder whether Sharen Wilson, the Republican district attorney who aggressively pursued the case, would have used peremptory strikes to ensure just that. In any case, I doubt that a fair jury, one that included black people and other POC, would have decided to send a mother to prison for mistakenly filling out a provisional ballot. Instead of a jury, Mason's fate was solely in the hands of District Judge Ruben Gonzalez (yes, name drops for the DA and judge), who decided that Mason should do five years' time for overlooking some fine print.

"It doesn't make any sense," Mason said in an

interview with *The Guardian*. "Why would I vote if I knew I was not eligible? What's my intent? What was I to gain by losing my kids, losing my mom, potentially losing my house? I have so much to lose, all for casting a vote." She appealed her sentence and was denied.

Meanwhile, in the very same county where Mason voted that year, a judge named Russ Casey pleaded guilty to turning in fake signatures to secure a place on a Texas primary ballot. His crime was not, in any way, an accident or oversight. It was a premeditated affront to our political system. Casey pleaded guilty to committing that crime, and for his guilty plea, the Texas courts sentenced him to two years in jail—then commuted his two-year prison sentence to a five-year sentence of probation. Can you believe that? A five-year sentence upheld on appeal for a black woman versus a two-year sentence commuted into probation for a white man. The Fix was in way back when. And the Fix is in right this second.

Talk It, Walk It

GO TO WWW.USA.GOV/ABSENTEE-VOTING to find out about mail-in voting in your state. You can find general information as well as a link to your state's local election office for specific rules in your state. You can also visit www.vote.org/polling-place-locator/ to find the polling stations in your state or community.

If you're in Texas, call your elected official and

demand that Crystal Mason be released from jail. If you're elsewhere, visit the American Civil Liberties Union, which, among other things, launches legal battles against voter suppression all over the country. Their website (aclu.org/issues/voting-rights/fighting -voter-suppression) has a whole tab of resources on the subject. While you're there, donate some money if your means allow it.

Volunteer at a local community organization or shelter, a place where you can encounter citizens who might not be as informed on the voting process and their particular voting rights. Help register voters, especially in areas with a high number of black people and/or POCs and/or poor people. Next election, work at a polling station and be as helpful as you possibly can, pointing out the fine print when necessary. Visit the League of Women Voters (LWV) website (lwv.org) and donate to them, too. Read up on the For the People Act, and then call up your state legislators and push them to vote for it. Visit the NAACP (naacp.org) and donate to some of their empowerment programs. You could also sign up as a volunteer to help turn out voters. Support black leadership, and remember to choose your leaders critically. Write an op-ed. Start a GoFundMe for someone's legal fees. As with systemic racism, the issues are countless, but so are the ways to help.

One more note: don't forget about local elections. State legislatures have a huge influence on what you can and can't do where you live; the mayor approves the city budget on things like police or school funding; your local district attorney has say over who goes to prison and who doesn't. Local elections can even get your potholes filled, and I think we're all anti-potholes. So do your research on the candidates just as you would for a president. Attend their speeches and debates when you can, call them out on issues of fairness and bias. Make them accountable to their records in a public forum. Also, make sure you always show up for jury duty when you're called. If you have people of color in your life, make sure they don't skirt jury duty either. Vote, vote, vote, vote like your life depends on it. Like our lives depend on it. They do.

"America claims to have abolished slavery generations ago. But with a lack of public investment in black communities directly contributing to high prison populations, and prisons often benefiting from the free labor of their inmates, did we ever truly abolish slave labor? Or has the 13th Amendment simply provided prison owners with a loophole?" —Eric

10.

THUG LIFE

Justice for Some

They kill or maim on impulse, without any
intelligible motive.... The buzz of impulsive
violence, the vacant stares and smiles, and
the remorseless eyes ... they quite literally
have no concept of the future.... They
place zero value on the lives of their victims,
whom they reflexively dehumanize ...
capable of committing the most heinous
acts of physical violence for the most trivial
reasons ... for as long as their youthful
energies hold out, they will do what comes
"naturally": murder, rape, rob, assault,
burglarize, deal deadly drugs, and get high.

—CRIMINOLOGIST JOHN DILULIO, COINING THE TERM
SUPERPREDATOR IN THE *WASHINGTON EXAMINER*, 1995

I didn't have any interaction with gangs myself when
I was growing up. But when I think about them
now, I think of the rough neighborhoods where many

black children grow up, of the news stories about the violence in those neighborhoods. When I hear *gang member*, I picture a boy in elementary school being asked what he wants to be when he grows up and him saying a lawyer or a doctor or an NFL player, but never saying a gang member. I think about how some people join gangs because they want to feel protected and how other people join them because it's what the family did.

That second reason reminds me of growing up in Texas. Around me, you either went to Texas or you went to Texas A&M—period. It was cultish. If you were driving around neighborhoods in Dallas, you might see a ton of the burnt-orange-and-white Longhorn flags in one yard, and in the yard next to it, you'd see the maroon-and-white Texas A&M flag: archrivals for life. If your parents went to the University of Texas, you'd better not even think about fixing your lips to go to Texas A&M. The schools were only an hour and a half from each other but might as well have been on opposite sides of the moon. I was a Longhorn, so I got busy hating A&M. In all honesty, I didn't know why; still don't. But to this day, if I hear somebody say, "Gig 'em, Aggies," which is Texas A&M's slogan, there's a visceral reaction of disgust in me. I was conditioned to see maroon and white and know that that was my enemy.

You might think where I'm going with this analogy is that this is how young men get drafted into gangs.

And yes, I could go there—but first, let's visit another scene where someone has decided to hate a group of people on the strength of inherited prejudice. It happened in the White House, where back in 1995 a Princeton professor and criminologist named John Dilulio was invited to attend a working dinner with President Clinton on juvenile crime. At that dinner, Dilulio introduced Clinton to a term he'd invented: the *superpredator*. See the beginning of the chapter for his, uh, colorful definition.

As you might imagine, Dilulio's description had a lot of people scared. And while he didn't say all superpredators were black, at that dinner and later, he did point out that trouble would be greatest in inner-city *black* neighborhoods and also took care to remind people that it would spill into the suburbs. That was bad, but maybe the most damaging thing Dilulio did was say that the kids were doing what came "naturally" to them, as if violence was coded in their DNA, as if there were a generation of young black sociopaths. Claiming the naturalness of black male violence aligned with our long history of vilifying them—remember the Angry Black Man, my friends.

Ugly as it was, the idea of the superpredator caught on. It had a champion in Hillary Clinton, who referenced it in a stump speech for her husband's anti-crime agenda. His goal, she said, was to take back the streets "from crime, gangs, and drugs":

And we have actually been making progress on this count as a nation. Because of what local law enforcement is doing. Because of what citizens and neighborhood patrols are doing . . . But we also need to have an organized effort against gangs. Just like we had an organized effort against the mob. We need to take these people on. They are often connected to big drug cartels. They are not just gangs of kids anymore. They are often the kinds of kids that are called super-predators. No conscience. No empathy. We can talk about why they ended up that way, but first we have to bring them to heel.

That same thinking had birthed President Clinton's now notorious 1994 crime bill, technically called the Violent Crime Control and Law Enforcement Act. This implemented things like a "three strikes" mandatory life sentence for repeat offenders, provided funding for hiring one hundred thousand new police officers, and also provided a whopping $9.7 billion for new prisons. It also expanded the kinds of offenses that could earn the death penalty. The bill, coupled with the image of the superpredator, helped create the conditions of mass incarceration we see today.

Friend, this chapter's another bumpy ride. The tricky thing with crime and punishment in the black community is that there is a lot of real, tragic violence being perpetrated, often against other black people— and too often dismissed as black-on-black crime, somehow less worthy of notice than the ever-feared black-on-white crime. This violence is, in itself, the product of systemic racism in ways we've already talked a bit about. At the same time, the policing and incarceration of black bodies is overblown and unjust, exacerbated in no small part by the racist specter of the superpredator, the gangbanger, the thug. It's time to untangle the reality from the fiction.

Let's Rewind

THE WAY PEOPLE talk about gang violence and street crime, you'd think black people invented the whole shebang. The Crips and Bloods and Latin Kings are infamous for a reason, but the first gangs in America were actually white people, formed shortly after the Revolutionary War. (One of the less-celebrated firsts.) After American immigration picked up in the 1800s, on-their-way-to-white gangs emerged. Remember *Gangs of New York*? Some experts call the Irish American group featured in that movie, the Five Points Gang, still the most significant gang in American history. And yet, somehow, white men as a whole have not been marred by their violence.

Black and Latinx folks didn't get into the gang scene at all until the early twentieth century and didn't really get cooking until the 1950s and '60s. The Crips and the Bloods are black gangs, both formed in poverty-stricken South Central LA. The Crips were formed in the late 1960s by guys named Raymond Washington and Tookie Williams and originally styled after the Black Panther Party—a black militant group fighting for civil rights. Back then, their role was to provide protection from other neighborhood gangs, as well as to combat police harassment. The Crips ruled the day for a few years until a rival gang named the Bloods was formed in Compton by high schoolers Sylvester Scott and Benson Owens. Gang violence from the 1970s into the early '80s was seldom lethal, but that changed with the crack cocaine epidemic of the 1980s, when Crips and Bloods got into drug trafficking. The cocktail of guns, drugs, and money wrought enough violence that by the late '80s, hundreds of gang murders were occurring each year.

I give you that history to say: that's the reality of the worst of the worst. Gangs as brutal, organized criminal enterprises. But, friends, there is so much in black communities, even among young men with gang ties, that is not that. Yet all black communities suffer the consequences of gang stereotypes.

In what might seem ironic, the term *black-on-black crime* was started by black people in the 1970s, particularly by people writing about crime in Chicago. Soon after, black leader Jesse Jackson started to chastise white government officials and the media for "their silence and ineffectiveness in dealing with the present black-on-black crime crisis." Jackson was actually complaining about the unfairness of the criminal justice system, how black people were being treated more harshly. Then a famous black psychiatrist named

Alvin F. Poussaint published a book titled *Why Blacks Kill Blacks* (it even had an intro by Jesse Jackson). By the 1980s, the term had been thrown around enough for it to stick in the public consciousness. It had also been transformed from well-intentioned black people decrying an unfair justice system and the products of systemic racism, to white people making the case that violence is endemic to black people and drafting policies that make the problem worse.

These days, the All Lives Matter crowd often trots out the statistic that the majority of black people are killed by black people and asks why black folks care about white-on-black crime—specifically, death by police officer—more than black-on-black crime. That's not the case. Black people care about being murdered. In addition to its murky genesis, *black-on-black crime* is a misleading term without context. The most important bit of context: that the majority of violent crimes against white people are perpetrated by white people. As sad as it may seem, people generally commit crimes against people of the same race. And I've never heard anyone in my life (have you?) reference white people killing white people as *white-on-white crime*.

You want to know the truth? Poverty, not race, is a more accurate predictor of who commits crimes. To the extent that black-on-black crime exists, it's the product of, among other systemic factors I've discussed, segregated housing, concentrated poverty, and unequal schooling. According to the Bureau for Justice Statistics, people living in households with income below the federal poverty line are twice as likely to commit violent crime than high-income households, regardless of race. We've been doing it wrong. The best tough-on-crime bill is a tough—the toughest—on-poverty bill.

Yes, there's an issue with crime in many black communities, and it certainly needs to be addressed. But what black people don't need and can't stand is the stigma that this is only a black problem. Let me say this, too: neither violent policing nor mass incarceration is the answer. You ever heard of the saying "Men lie, women lie, but numbers don't"? Well, check out some of the statistics from the report *An Unjust Burden: The Disparate Treatment of Black Americans in the Criminal Justice System*:

- **Black men comprise about 13 percent of the U.S. male population, but nearly 35 percent of all men who are under state or federal jurisdiction with a sentence of more than one year.**

- **One in three black men born in 2001 can expect to be incarcerated in his lifetime, compared to 1 in 6 Latino men and 1 in 17 white men.**

- **Black people are incarcerated in state prisons at a rate 5.1 times greater than that of white people.**

- **One in 18 black women born in 2001 will be incarcerated sometime in her life, compared to 1 in 45 Latina women and 1 in 111 white women.**

- **Forty-four percent of incarcerated women are black, although black women make up about 13 percent of the female U.S. population.**

It's easy to say that black people—black men especially—are being over-policed. The above spells it out in hard data. And this isn't something out of the blue but from the predictable outcomes of years of racist policies.

NOW THAT WE have this background, I want to get into something you may encounter on the regular. If you've heard anyone talk about gangs and violence, you may have heard them use the word *thug*. Every once in a while, which is still too often, it gets thrown around in football. After an ill-advised on-the-field postgame interview during the 2013 NFC Championship, Richard Sherman, who was playing for the Seahawks at the time, went off about receiver Michael Crabtree. Shoot, he probably wasn't even out of the locker room before he got the ire of Twitter and all kinds of sports message boards turned on him. Some of those people were calling him a *thug*. Sherman, who apologized later for his interview, took offense at the label. He likened people using the word *thug* to describe him as a new way of calling black people the N-word. Sherman's a smart dude, a Stanford grad, and I have to say, the man had a point.

Sherman wasn't the first, nor sadly will he be the

last black man to be called a thug. If you sift through your memory, I bet you can remember other instances of black people being called *thugs*, have heard police or a politician use *thug* to describe a black man in the inner city, or an aggressive protestor or an athlete, like Sherman, who steps out of the bounds of what sports fans deem normal.

It actually comes from the Hindi word *thuggee*, which means "deceiver" or "thief" or "swindler." Thugs stole and murdered in India for more than five hundred years. The word didn't catch on in America until Mark Twain wrote about them in the 1800s, in work that colored the word with the connotation of a gangster. Back then, white people had American thugism on straight lock. (Remember, black people were still enslaved or, in other words, they didn't possess the freedom to even be thugs.) But since *thug* always had a negative connotation, and since black people from the jump have been associated with negative stereotypes, it was easy to paint them as thugs post-emancipation and for it to catch on.

Now I'm not going to sit here and say that the term doesn't fit the behavior of some people, black people included, but I also want you to remember something when you hear people using it. Calling someone a thug is putting them on a continuum that ends with a superpredator. It's a way of saying: this is what you *are*, not just what you do—or more often, what other people who look like you have done.

A thug is the fictional archetype of Dilulio's nightmares, a stand-in for a black man that is hopelessly lost to violence or drugs; a vector of crime that needs to be feared and stopped; a caricature instead of a human being. And that kind of thinking is not what we need to fix either gang violence *or* over-policing in this country.

The bottom line: our criminal justice system too often treats black people like thugs instead of like people. So the cycle perpetuates, and both stereotypes and actual violence keep going and going and going.

Let's Get Uncomfortable

FIRST, A FINAL THOUGHT on *thug*. Just as with the N-word, black people do our best to take some of the sting out of it. You know the old saying "If you can't run from it, run into it"? It's like that.

I didn't grow up on Tupac or Biggie (actually, my parents were jamming to that Nigerian gospel music), but I've seen pictures of Tupac's THUG LIFE tattooed on his stomach. I've heard old songs from the group Bone Thugs-n-Harmony (them brothers could sing!). These days, there's Slim Thug and Young Thug, and I'm sure some other Thug-named rappers I don't even know about. Go ahead and listen to them, go ahead and tell people Slim Thug's your fave. Just don't go calling people *thugs*.

As for the crime stuff. Trust me, I get it. No one

wants to knowingly put themselves in danger. America is steeped in stereotypes about the danger of black men, and when those mingle with the real statistics of disproportionate black arrests and incarceration, it can be hard to know what to believe when you're debating whether to cross the street in front of the guy in the hoodie. But you also have to consider many of the things I've been talking about in this book. We can't have the stereotype of black men as inherently dangerous without President Wilson thinking *Birth of a Nation* was "like history written in lightning," without all the lies and propaganda used to lynch black men, without black people being maligned as superpredators.

This book isn't going to make you all of a sudden lose all of your biases. But for those of you who wonder whether you'll be able to evolve your thinking, I offer Hillary Clinton as an example. In 2016—at a fundraiser for her own presidential campaign—Clinton was confronted by a Black Lives Matter activist named Ashley Williams. "I'm not a superpredator, Hillary Clinton. Can you apologize to black people for mass incarceration?" Williams said, while brandishing a sign that quoted Clinton's old words back to her: "We have to bring them to heel." Williams didn't get out much more than that before the $500-a-head donors started shushing her, and the Secret Service escorted her out of the building. Williams also didn't get an answer from Clinton that day.

But thank goodness for the viral cell phone videos. People saw the confrontation, and journalists started writing about it. And, wouldn't you know it, in a *Washington Post* interview a few days later, Williams and black people got their apology from Clinton: "In that speech, I was talking about the impact violent crime and vicious drug cartels were having on communities across the country and the particular danger they posed to children and families," said Clinton. "Looking back, I shouldn't have used those words, and I wouldn't use them today."

Talk It, Walk It

THE NEXT TIME you hear someone mention black-on-black crime, educate them that it's a myth. You might start with a question: Do you know where the term black-on-black crime came from? Also, here's a language-born mindset change: instead of thinking of it as criminal justice, think of it as justice. We get into sticky territory with the word *criminal*. Not that criminals don't exist, but who gets called a criminal and why is not so cut-and-dried and usually has something to do with race and class or both. Along those same lines, again, try to stop using the word *thug*, even as a joke. I hope I've made clear how harmful it can be. As the philosopher Norman Vincent Peale used to say, "Change your thoughts and change your world."

Visit the Sentencing Project (sentencingproject .org). There's a bunch of information on how you can get involved with justice reform. You can even select your state and see what current reforms are being proposed. You should also check out the Marshall Project (themarshallproject.org), which is a journalism site focused on justice reform and reimagining the role of police in public safety. I also invite you to visit Pen American (pen.org) and read some of the wonderful writing coming out of prisons. If you're interested in the humanity of people who are incarcerated, who better to educate you than people actually in prison?

Two classic films that really get into the nuances of gangs and so-called thugs are John Singleton's *Boyz n the Hood* and the Hughes Brothers' *Menace II Society*. If you're really interested in understanding the plight of young black men in gangs, check out them both. Also try the Ava DuVernay miniseries *When They See Us*, about the miscarriage of justice known as the trial of the Central Park Five.

Call up your representative and let them know that you stand for responsible justice policies. Two timely causes to consider advocating: protecting the incarcerated from COVID-19, and the Second Look legislation, which proposes reevaluating for possible release people who have served long prison sentences and have aged out of committing crimes.

"Why do you think many African American communities are plagued with poverty, crime, and also the lack of presence of a father figure in the home? Is this all because of oppression?" —Lisa

11.

PICKING UP THE PIECES

The Black Family Struggle

The breakdown of the black community, in order to maintain slavery, began with the breakdown of the black family. Men and women were not legally allowed to get married because you couldn't have that kind of love. It might get in the way of the economics of slavery. Your children could be taken from you and literally sold down the river.

–KERRY WASHINGTON

I want to start by acknowledging that this chapter is the hardest one for me to write. That's because it's the furthest from my own personal experience. I'm like most of you reading this, assuming you fall under the majority of white people (76 percent) in America who grow up in two-parent homes or with the presence of both parents in your life. That's how I grew up: with both Mom and Dad around. My dad only ever missed one football game in my entire playing career from high school and college. I know my dad only ever missed one football game because he only ever missed *one* football game. I saw my mom go back and get her doctoral degree in her fifties, something that inspired me, encouraged me, taught me that I didn't have any excuses. The reason I don't drink is because I never saw my dad drink. The reason that I rarely curse is because I never heard my parents curse. I know my parents are the reason I am who I am.

That said, one of my best friends from the NFL is Earl Wolff. My dog Earl is from Fayetteville, North Carolina. His parents separated when he was around seven, and after that, his pops didn't play much of a role in his life. But Earl still found his way to NC State to play football (he played safety and is one of the all-time leading tacklers at his position) and was then drafted to the NFL, where we played together on the Eagles. He grew up with his mom, Sharon, and his sweet grandmother Grace. I went to Earl's family's house for Thanksgiving one year—I can still taste the sweet potatoes, the collard greens, the pumpkin pie, and the wings and the mac and cheese . . . mmm-hmm, those ladies knew how to throw down. It was the bomb.

Meals aside, though, I asked Earl how it had felt growing up in a single-parent home. He said his mom had to play the role of both a mom and a dad but that this had also made his mom his best friend. During Earl's freshman, sophomore, and senior year at NC State, Sharon went to every one of his college football games. She always sat in the same spot in the stands, except for his junior year, when she wasn't there because she was stationed in Kuwait.

Sharon had joined the military to provide for her family, and that's why she went to Kuwait, too—it wasn't a military order but a financial decision. She wanted to make sure her kids were taken care of. The whole time she was overseas, Earl told me, when he didn't hear from her for a while, he'd be scared to death. Once, while waiting to hear from her, he just started crying, because he knew she could be gone at a moment's notice. Earl's mom put her life at risk every day to make sure her kids could eat. And while he told me he didn't have any regrets about being raised in a single-parent household, I kept thinking that if his mother had had a partner during his junior year, that partner could've shouldered some of the financial burden. Earl would not have had to play his junior year wondering if his mother would be killed.

Earl and I came from totally different family structures, but we got to the same place. I'm not here to say that anybody can't make good coming from any background, nor am I here to say that the women who raised my friend didn't do an amazing job. That said, we have to talk about what black families go through. Black families have much higher rates of single-parent homes. Those single-parent homes mean less income and a greater risk of poverty. Those homes also produce higher dropout rates, higher teenage pregnancy rates, and greater chances of being involved in the justice system—and a host of other negative outcomes. The point is not that broken families are bad: that's obvious. The question is, who has done the breaking, and how have they done it?

Let's Rewind

I WANT TO take you way back, in this case, to twenty-four years before slavery ended. Below is the transcript of a letter from one Cecar Pugh, a free "man of colour," to a slaveholder in North Carolina, the state where he'd been formerly enslaved. The letter, which we have to admit is well written for someone forbidden to read and write for part of his life, inquires about the possibility of buying one of his own grandsons to care for him in his old age:

> **South Carolina Anderson District Nov. 29th 1841**
> Dear Sir—you will please to excuse me for venturing to address you inasmuch as the subject

may be uninterresting to you but of interest to myself—I am told that you own a black woman named Harriett & her family of children it is said & I believe that she is my child and the only one I have alive I wish her to know that I am injoying reasonable health & intends to come and [see] her as soon as I can make it convenient and if it suits you & her I want one of her sons to take care of me in this my decline of life and I am willing to pay a fair price for him if you will let me have him and be so condesending and let me know immediately write by mail and dirict your letter to Henry Cobb Esqr. Golden Grove post office Greenville Dist S-C.

My name is Cecar was borned & raired near Winsor & formerly belong to the Pugh family— Harrietts mother was named Patsy & belong to Doctor Darby if you please write to me and Dirict as above stated & let me know whether you will let me have one of her children or not & what will be the price & what kind of money would suit you in payment. I dont know the given name but suppose it to be john or James

Yours with respect Signed, Cecar Pugh
A Man of Colour

[Courtesy of the State Archives of North Carolina]

Note that he calls himself a free man of color—the use of "man" implying a free man—but is searching for an enslaved daughter. Can you imagine living as a free person but knowing your daughter, your grandchildren, were still in bondage? Notice that he's looking for his daughter but doesn't know her last name.

Now imagine circumstances under which one of your parents wouldn't know your last name. He doesn't even know his grandson's first name: again, imagine that's your grandfather. And let's not forget that he's trying to buy his grandson to help take care of himself. Does this mean he's been indoctrinated to see his own kin as property now?

I started with this letter because we just can't talk about the phenomenon of broken black families without the context of slavery. Remember that, legally, enslaved people were property, not persons. They therefore couldn't enter into contracts, including marriage contracts. Enslaved people still entered into non-"legal" unions, but these were always precarious. If the husband was owned by one person and the wife and children another, it was called an *abroad marriage*. A father might walk several miles to see his wife and children on Wednesday or Saturday evening, given that all his work was done for his master. Some owners would let people choose their partners, while others would arrange marriages, forcing people into pairs they wouldn't have chosen themselves. As far as family life went, women would return to work soon after they'd delivered a baby, and by the time the kids reached school age—though there was no schooling—they were put to work: fanning flies from the owner's table, taking care of their owner's younger children, running errands, and eventually working in the fields like their parents. There was no such thing as breadwinning for a father, of course, as all his labor was for the benefit of someone else. And if the mothers were not working in the fields, they were working in the house, and/or raising the children of white people. If a family somehow managed to overcome those obstacles to approximate a marriage and family, there was always the threat that an owner would break apart that family.

Following the Civil War, thousands of black people set out to reunite with their families, some of them crossing half a continent in searching. Hundreds placed advertisements in newspapers and sent letters to the Freedmen's Bureau, searching for wives, husbands, children, and other family members who'd been sold off. Some parents returned to places from which they'd been sold to retrieve their children. In a few cases, when people who'd been sold elsewhere and started up new families were found by old families, they created combined families to keep everybody together. Thousands of formerly enslaved black people formalized their marriages.

It remained an uphill battle to unite and keep families together for many, many years.

Before I go any further, a few words on the worst of all arguments: that this is just how black families are. As if black people are genetically disposed to this brokenness. If broken families were in the nature of black people, how do we explain all those efforts in the wake of war? How to explain why black people didn't have broken families when they were back in

Africa? As an African and first-generation American, I can confidently say that in Nigeria, family ties are every bit as strong, if not stronger, than they are here. If this book has emphasized anything, it's that history has a huge part to play on what kind of America we live in now. What we see of the black family is the legacy of America's first black families. So if the brokenness isn't inherent, why has that legacy persisted for so long?

Black people were promised "forty acres and a mule" after the war, and most of them never got it. (President Andrew Johnson reneged on it.) What they got instead were Black Codes, laws that restricted them in most areas of life while also making it possible for former slave owners to rehire them. Many black people worked as sharecroppers, which was basically slave-master relations updated to peasant–feudal lord status. Lots of scholars argue that you can draw a straight line between the too-many black single-parent households today and the severe economic hardship after emancipation. Mothers ended up having to work instead of staying home and raising children. Fathers were either out of work or forced into this new kind of slave labor, sharecropping. The resources for schooling were also, needless to say, subpar. These impoverished conditions lasted for decades.

In 1965, Daniel Patrick Moynihan, then the U.S. assistant secretary of labor, published *The Negro*

Family: The Case for National Action, also known as *The Moynihan Report*. It looked at the link between black poverty and family structure. Moynihan wrote that the breakdown of the black nuclear family was hindering progress toward equality. That report became, per *The Atlantic*, "one of the most controversial documents of the 20th century." Liberals argued that it advocated for policies to fix raced-based inequalities, while conservatives called for bootstrapping—by people who, by and large, had no boots—and/or used the report to reinforce stereotypes about loose family morality in black families.

Three years later, in 1968, President Lyndon Johnson appointed a committee to investigate racial divisions. The National Advisory Commission on Civil Disorders, better known as the Kerner Commission, issued a blistering report on the state of race relations in America. (The bureaucrats love a report!) Its most famous lines: "Our nation is moving toward two societies, one black, one white—separate and unequal." *The Kerner Report* had a lot to say on the media's role in this:

> The media had too long basked in a white world, looking out of it, if at all, with white men's eyes and a white perspective. Researchers consistently point to a pattern of news selection and coverage that represents the views and values of the homogenous world of journalists . . . the social order of public, business, and professional,

upper-middle-class, middle-aged, and white male sectors of society.

Take a look at your local newscast. Take note of how black people and people of color are being portrayed. I bet what you'll see are extremes: athletes and entertainers portrayed as demigods, other black people portrayed as poor or violent or criminal. What you will see are black people as victims of violence and poverty or feel-good stories noting the great achievements of the first black such-and-such. Imagine the whiplash, the parallel messaging about possibilities for the future to any young black children watching. All likely reported in a voice, that standard (white) American news voice, that doesn't resemble their experience at all.

Today, as much as in 1968, Americans are told again and again of the broken black family, such that many white people believe it's our natural state. Meanwhile, those messages erode the esteem of black people. Someone with healthy esteem may be able to, say, ignore people assuming they have no father figure or overcome the real obstacles of that situation. But what about the person who never sees relatable images of themselves, who doesn't hear themselves on TV, who begins to disbelieve in their worth as a human being? How does that person become a positive member of a healthy family? They may not.

If you told me, in any given year, that I had a

one-in-four chance of winning a Super Bowl, I would've been stoked. But here's a one-in-four statistic that's way less appealing: about one in four black Americans will experience an anxiety disorder at some point in their life. Researchers say black people that experience chronic racism can develop something called *racial battle fatigue*, a state that includes, among other symptoms, anxiety, worry, hypervigilance, headaches, and increased heart rate and blood pressure. A study by the National Comorbidity Survey Replication and the National Survey of American Life found that almost one in ten black people actually have PTSD. Yeah, the same disorder that happens to soldiers at war. And whether it's PTSD or something else, black people are 20 percent more likely than white people to suffer serious psychological distress. Suicide is the third leading cause of death for black people ages fifteen to twenty-four, and black men are at four times higher risk than black women.

I don't mean to fill your head with more numbers, and I know these are particularly bleak—but I want you to have a sense of just how much of a toll everything we've talked about is having on black folks. It's tougher to keep a family together when you're fighting for your mental health, if not your life. Oh, and it's a recap at this point, but let's not forget the unequal education system, the stereotypes that vilify young black men, the justice system that forms a prison pipeline, discrimination in hiring, and for good measure, those racist housing practices. All those things work to-gether to destabilize black people, making it harder and harder to keep families intact.

Let's Get Uncomfortable

I'M NOT TRYING to guilt you. Seriously. But I am try-ing to put this idea of broken black families in context, and that means asking what role whiteness has played in the breaking. It means, as with every chapter in this book, looking and listening harder.

As I mentioned, I grew up in a strong two-parent home and mostly saw the same kinds of families as mine growing up. But I got to see some effects of the black family struggle when I went to college, where so many of my black teammates were either raised by single moms or raised by their grandparents. I re-member on recruiting visits, I'd see a white recruit stroll in with their two parents, blithe as anything. And then I'd see a black recruit stroll in with only his mom. Once we became teammates, I got to hear sto-ries about what it was like for them growing up, and it was so much different from my life. While it made me thankful for my parents and for the resources and ex-ample that they provided me, it hurt me to hear what happened with kids who never knew their fathers, or whose fathers were killed or went to prison, to know guys whose mothers struggled with addiction or who had to grow up on welfare. I now know so much more about the pain of my black brothers and sisters and how much more black children have to work to over-come and defy the odds.

We all need to work together to make sure those odds are better.

Talk It, Walk It

THE NEXT TIME you hear someone spouting off about broken black families, make sure you help contextualize the issue for them. Talk about the history of black families and slavery. Talk about how the media portrays black people and the way that shapes all of our perceptions. Talk about systemic racism.

Another language shift for you: I've used *broken* in this chapter because it's so prevalent, but I don't love it for the same reason I use *enslaved* rather than *slave*. To call it a *broken black family* makes it seems like the brokenness is somehow normal, just how black families are—when we know by now that the disjoint owes a lot to systemic forces. What if we called them *broken-apart* families instead? That would put more emphasis on the fact that black families didn't become fractured all on their own. Think on it, my friends.

To help black families around you, visit the Big Brothers Big Sisters (www.bbbs.org) or the National Mentoring Resource Center (www .nationalmentoringresourcecenter.org) and sign up to be a mentor of young black people. Donate time or resources to an underfunded school near you. Ask your job to direct some of its corporate giving to a nonprofit program that works with at-risk youth or single parents.

If you want more context, read *The Moynihan Report* and *The Kerner Report*. Ask yourself how much has changed since the 1960s. And please, support black art—books, music, TV, films, visual art—especially that which provides nuanced images and characterizations of black people. I recommend James Baldwin's novel *If Beale Street Could Talk* and the Barry Jenkins film adaptation, a great characterization of how black families endured in the '50s and '60s against stacked odds. Tell your friends when you like something. As more of these projects become profitable, more of them will exist in the world. The more that exist, the greater likelihood of nuanced depictions of black people. The more nuanced the depictions, the better to combat harmful stereotypes, the greater the chance of broadening perspectives about black people.

Part III

"I am a white man who is married to a black woman, and we have two beautiful children. Being a white man, I cannot begin to know the pressures of being black in America. As a father to interracial children, I fear that I cannot adequately prepare them for the future. How can I explain to my son and daughter that life could be harder for them than it was for me?" —Kevin

12.

LOVE WINS
The Interracial Family

My journey of love can't be any different
just because of the color of someone's
skin. And people can't judge me for picking
someone who doesn't look like me. I feel
like they expect me to pick someone who
looks just like me, but that's not fair. They
should want me to fall in love with whoever
it is that I vibe with.

—RACHEL LINDSAY

I recently had two interracial couples on my show:
Rachel Lindsay and Bryan Abasolo from season
13 of *The Bachelorette*, and Olympic gold medalist
Lindsey Vonn and P. K. Subban, a star defenseman
for the New Jersey Devils. I hit them with a question one of my viewers had asked me, which was, do
I as a black man feel betrayed when I see a black
woman with a white man? I've been confronted

with how I feel about that kind of relationship many times. And what I said then, and am saying now, is that I don't feel betrayed, but I do feel a little unsettled—a little curious as to what's going on there.

Was it weird to hear that? Stay with me, because we gonna get uncomfortable. First, though, I want to take stock of where we are. So far, this book has been mostly about the divide between black and white Americans, which is necessary for a book about race and racism. As a reminder, "I don't see color" is not an okay thing to say, because to say we're all exactly the same is to gloss over a whole history and presence of inequality. That's why the first two parts of the book were called "You and Me" and "Us and Them"—because to get anywhere with these uncomfortable conversations, we had to acknowledge that we're starting from different places. This last part is called "We," because now that we've addressed some of our differences of experience and gaps in (white) understanding—there's also so much room for black and white Americans to work together, to understand and empathize with each other's humanity.

This chapter is all about the very front lines of "We": interracial families and relationships. So what is it really like, in all its worthwhile challenges, to build a life across our country's oldest divide?

Let's Rewind

RIGHT BEFORE CHRISTMAS of 1863, a pamphlet appeared on newsstands, titled *Miscegenation: The Theory of the Blending of the Races, Applied to the American White Man and Negro*. First, that's a superlong title. Okay, now to the important stuff. The authors coined *miscegenation* from the Latin words *miscere* (to mix) and *genus* (race), and the pamphlet was actually a parody, only pretending to endorse white and black people having babies together. "The miscegenetic or mixed races are much superior, mentally, physically, and morally, to those pure or unmixed," wrote the pamphlet's anonymous authors, later discovered as two anti-abolitionist journalists. You can imagine how that language was received in the midst of the Civil War. Trolling's been around a long time, y'all.

The reality beneath this pamphlet's "joke" was that in addition to being seen as "less than" under slavery and beyond, black people were also in some ways seen as exotic, as mysteriously "other" bodies to be fetishized by white men and women. White men (it was almost always men) acted on those perceptions often enough that as early as 1662, southern colonies applied what was called the *one-drop rule*, also known as *hypodescent*. That rule stipulated that a baby's race was determined by its mother, which was another way of saying that white men fornicating with or raping their slaves couldn't produce freedom for their offspring. After the war ended and black people were legally set free, miscegenation became not just about banning sex but about marriage, too. Both of these bans were, at heart, about protecting the most important part of chattel slavery: the number of human bodies available for the labor.

Marriage between white people and black people was officially outlawed by *Pace v. Alabama* in 1883. In that infamous Supreme Court decision, the court unanimously upheld the conviction of a black man and white woman who'd been sentenced to two years' imprisonment for violating Alabama's miscegenation law, setting a precedent for banning interracial marriages all over the country. *Eighty years later*, a serious challenge came up, when a black-white interracial couple in Florida was threatened with a year in prison for the charge of "race-contingent fornication," a.k.a. living together as an unmarried couple (because they couldn't get married). Their case (*McLaughlin v. Florida*) made it to the Supreme Court in 1964, and the court ruled in the couple's favor.

That verdict made way for the coup de grâce: *Loving v. Virginia* in 1967. In that case, a white man and a black woman appealed Virginia's rejection of their marriage all the way to the Supreme Court, which ruled (shout-out to the ACLU) that so-called anti-miscegenation laws were unconstitutional. Wrote Chief Justice Earl Warren, "Under our Constitution, the freedom to marry, or not marry, a person of another race resides with the individual, and cannot be infringed by the state." It was a great day for black-white love, but here's a little perspective on that victory: black people had received both their civil and voting rights before they were allowed to legally marry white people.

Another way people have built families across racial lines is through adoption. To understand what's called *transracial adoption*, first a beat on adoption itself. In 1851, Massachusetts passed the Adoption of Children Act, recognizing it as a legal operation based on a child's welfare (rather than, say, to avoid the stigma of having a kid out of wedlock) and therefore required the parents to be "fit and proper." Back then, most adoptions adhered to the concept of *matching*. The goal was to set up families that would "match" families made naturally, and you know where this is going. Matching required that adoptive parents be married heterosexual couples who looked, felt, and behaved as if they'd conceived other people's children themselves. Whatever that meant, there weren't many kids of different races being adopted by white families.

The first instance on record of a white family adopting a black kid was in Minnesota in 1948, after which the practice became known as a *transracial adoption*. This still refers to any adoptive family with children of a different culture or race, but to be true, it's almost always nonwhite kids and white adults. And as you might guess, it's stirred up some opposition. Some of the strongest critics have been black organizations; for example, a group of social workers in the 1970s who took "a vehement stand against placements of black children in white homes for any reason." They called it "unnecessary," "unnatural," and "artificial," as well as proof positive that black people were still considered "chattel." For years, that kind of opposition put a serious slowdown on transracial adopting. Back then, as well, most adoptions were closed, meaning that the child and/or the new parents could not find out the identity of the birth parent. These days most adoptions have some degree of openness, meaning that there is at least some personal link with a child's heritage.

Let's Get Uncomfortable

SO AS WE'VE just seen, the history of interracial relationships and families in this country is . . . complicated. And just as it's tough to start a new relationship with a bunch of emotional baggage, it's tough to shrug all that off, no matter who you are.

When I see a black man with a white woman or a white woman with a black man, it's not so much that it bothers me, as it makes me curious. When I see them, I think, *How did y'all end up here?* I remind myself that, historically speaking, white people don't love black people. So even if your partner loves you, her parents maybe don't. Or if her mom and dad love you, her grandma and granddad probably don't love you. Or auntie and uncles and them don't love you. I also just wonder what's going on behind the scenes. If I'm honest, sometimes it is like, *Was a black man not good enough for you, black woman?* or *Was a black woman not good enough for you, black man?*

Those thoughts might be jarring for you to hear. Take a moment and sit with what I've shared. I don't think I'm alone in the sight of black-white interracial couples stirring something in me, but I need you to know that acknowledging that feeling is only the beginning. We have to talk about it if we are going to make progress toward real equality, toward a place where racism isn't defining so much of our world. We need to ask ourselves, how do we feel when we see an interracial couple? And why do we feel that way? We need to ask ourselves, how much of what we feel has been handed down to us from our parents and families, our friends, from history? These are questions we avoid, which says to me they are the questions worth asking and answering.

Here's my realest opinion: I believe a person should be able to love who they love. I believe that love wins. I believe a family can look however it looks and still be a family. With that in mind, some advice for treating everyone's heart with care:

If you're going to be in a relationship with a black person, please don't pick them because you think they're exotic. Ask yourself, really search yourself for the reasons you want to be with that person (as you would do with any prospective partner, but same-race relationships don't face anywhere near the same cultural scrutiny). Beware of tokenizing them, too. If your partner is the only black person in your life, that's a signal of trouble. On the flip side, take care to determine that you aren't being fetishized, exoticized, or tokenized. Let me help you out with a few smart questions to ask yourself before entering an interracial relationship: Is the privilege of the white partner understood? How does their family react to your relationship? How do their friends react? If you are religious, how does that affect your relationship? Would it be easier to date inside your own race? Why or why not?

If you're going to be in a relationship with a black person, be aware that your interracial relationship might include two different cultures and/or two different value systems. While you can ask about their values, don't expect a partner to educate you on their culture. If you care about them, you'll pursue that education yourself. Also, it's good to be curious, but try to be curious without making assumptions. Preconceived assumptions are prejudice, and you don't want to be prejudiced against your partner.

The least you can do is to see their color. As we've discussed, to be color blind is to not fully see a person, and in this case, that someone would be a person you strongly care about. To be color blind would be to ignore many of the things that make them particular. On a practical note, try to find friends who are also involved in interracial relationships. They can be a helpful sounding board for the issues you will face—and believe me, you will face issues. If you're really stuck, consider a relationship coach. Make sure you do your due diligence in researching the coach and verify that they have experience with interracial relationships.

Knowing about the culture of your loved one is a must in adoption, too. If you're going to adopt a black child, please make sure that you are versed in black culture. A rock-bottom start: learn little things as culturally specific as how to play spades and dominoes; see classic films like *The Wiz*, *School Daze*, *Malcolm X*, and *Coming to America*, as well as more contemporary ones like *Friday*, *The Wood*, *Love & Basketball*, and *Black Panther*. Take them to a black barbershop or hair salon; stay awhile.

And remember that not only does a black child need to know their black culture, they need to know their black history. You can't shield your child from the world for all of their life. Eventually, they are going to be in a world that isn't color blind. And they will have to know how to navigate that world that sees their color (or if they can pass, to choose how and when they want to express their heritage). While we will keep working toward ridding the world of racism, there will always be people who will see their color and judge them harshly or unfairly because of it. Better to prepare a child for that likely inevitability and to show them the world in all its context and complexity.

Talk It, Walk It

GROUND YOURSELF IN the history of interracial relationships in America. Start with the relationship between Thomas Jefferson and Sally Hemings, maybe the most famous interracial relationship of all time. If you're really interested in the roots of American perspectives on this, read the pamphlet I mentioned at the opening of this chapter: *Miscegenation: The Theory of the Blending of the Races, Applied to the American White Man and Negro.*

For more on transracial adoption, check out the documentary *Black, White & Us,* which follows four white families who have adopted black children. Another one to put on your to-watch list is *Closure,* which is about a woman who was transracially adopted by white parents. You might also check out the website Mashup Americans (mashupamericans.com), which has a heap of info on blended/mash-up families and in particular has advice for people considering transracial adoption. You can also find helpful info at AdoptUSKids (adoptuskids.org).

To end this chapter, I want to leave you with this. My favorite instrument to play is piano. I taught myself how to play in college, in breaks between training camp practices when there wasn't enough time to nap. Turned out, I loved it. During the most grueling parts of my time in the NFL, it kept me calm. Every day getting back from practice I would hop on my keyboard for a while. I still play even now. When I bought my first home in Austin, the first thing I purchased was a piano.

The beautiful thing about the piano is that you got white keys and you got black keys. And the only way to make the most beautiful, magnificent, and poetic noise is with both sets of keys working in tandem. You can't just play all white keys, because you won't maximize what the instrument has to offer. You can't just play all black keys, because you won't maximize what the instrument has to offer. But integrate the white and black keys together, and that is when the piano makes a joyful noise.

That's what this "we" is all about. If we can truly integrate white people and black people together, working in tandem, that's when our world will make its joyful noise.

"Why aren't the people obeying direct orders from police? Why are they resisting arrest? Any light you could shed on this would be greatly appreciated." —E.

13.

GOOD TROUBLE
Fighting for Change

The arc of the moral universe is long, but it
bends toward justice.

—DR. MARTIN LUTHER KING JR.

We must come to see that human progress
never rolls in on the wheels of inevitability.
It comes through the tireless efforts and the
persistent work of dedicated individuals
who are willing to be co-workers with
God. And without this hard work, time itself
becomes an ally of the primitive forces of
social stagnation. So we must help time and
realize that the time is always ripe to do
right.

—DR. MARTIN LUTHER KING JR.

During the protests in LA following the death of
George Floyd, my friend told me a story. He
said he was marching down Sunset Boulevard, past

white people holding up their signs, past black people holding up their signs, past people holding hands and marching in unison, and almost everyone was wearing their masks because of COVID-19. He looked to the right and saw a group of young black people.

"We're going down to Melrose and rob some people," one of them said. "We got to get them!"

My friend was like, "Uh, I got bad knees from playing ball. And, uh, I had a couple MCL tears and a couple meniscus surgeries, so, um, I'm gonna have to take a pass, y'all." He let the black dudes go and kept on marching. A little later, he came upon some white people who were trying to take a photo and arguing about the best pose for Instagram.

"Here, hold the sign like this," one said.

"No, no, no, like this," the other said.

My boy, who's a master of ceremonies and does a lot of writing about peace and unity, said that was it for him. He thought to himself, *Man, let me just go home and write something. Everybody has a different way of fighting, and my pen is my sword.*

My friend's story reminds me of something that happened in my own family. Twelve-year-old me had just finished putting on my school uniform—gray slacks, white button-down, black shoes with white socks—when all of a sudden, I heard crying and screaming from downstairs. I ran down and saw my mother throwing herself into our living room wall. I mean this literally; she was hurling her own body at the wall, shoulder-first. It hurt to see. What was going on?

My dad told me that my mom's sister had died in Nigeria. I knew that my mom throwing herself into a wall wasn't going to bring her sister back, and I guessed she knew that, too. It would take me years to process what was really happening. It took me learning about the five stages of grief: denial, anger, bargaining, depression, acceptance (FYI: not everyone goes through all the stages or experiences them in order). What I came to realize was that my mom was experiencing the anger stage of grief and that she didn't know what to do with her anger, so she beat it against a wall.

Have you ever been angry and not known what to do with it? I know it's happened to me. I've learned anger isn't always logical; shoot, it's probably illogical most of the time. And because of that, it's something we often don't know how to express. So what about when this happens not to one person but a group? What about when this happens to a whole lot of black people? When you see people out protesting for George Floyd, or Ahmaud Arbery, or Breonna Taylor, or any of our beloved black people who have been murdered, what you're seeing is a group of people who are angry. About police violence, about systemic inequality, about the American dream that isn't yet real for everyone. The protests take a lot of different forms, and even when they get violent—which I don't condone—what's really happening is just like my mother banging her shoulder against the wall.

The scenes of looting and destruction that so often light up the news and certain political rhetoric . . . they're only one end of the spectrum of black responses to the anger and frustration we've felt. An objectively small end at that. The LA protests weren't defined by that group of dudes going down to Melrose any more than a stadium of one hundred thousand football fans is defined by the few who have a drunken brawl in the parking lot. So in this chapter, I'd like to consider the full range of my brothers' and sisters' cries against racism in this country, from MLK to BLM. Black people all know a change needs to come, and are all figuring out how to fight for it.

I've had a million questions running through my own mind lately. Like, are protests necessary to effect change? Like, what are the most effective forms? Like, when does a "protest" become a "riot," and who gets to decide? And is there some line when a riot against injustice becomes something else—a rebellion? Let's get into what I've learned.

Let's Rewind

AMERICAN PROTEST PREDATES the United States of America. You can't talk protest in these United States without mentioning the Sons of Liberty rebelling against taxation without representation by throwing all those chests of tea into the Boston Harbor, or (some decades later) Nat Turner leading a rebellion of enslaved people in Virginia. The years since have seen a lot of ideas about what protest, justified and unjustified, looks like.

As always, the words we use matter, and I want to focus on four of them here: *protest*, *riot*, *rebellion*, and *massacre*. When it comes to the fight against racism in this country, an ongoing question has been who gets to decide which is which, and then how they get to enforce those decisions. You may think the lines are pretty clear: a protest is generally understood as an orderly demonstration; a riot, not so much; a rebellion is an uprising; and a massacre is, well, a massacre—a tragedy of one-sided violence. And yet, as with so much else, it turns out that race has played a big part in how protests are viewed. And policed.

Unpacking these words a bit more, Henry David Thoreau coined the term *civil disobedience*—still the gold standard for nonviolent protest everywhere. He described it as people prioritizing their conscience over the dictates of laws and expressing their grievances with civility. In plain speak, this meant people's consciences inspiring them to protest, but with manners. Civility is the key word in Thoreau's definition. To help get an understanding of what's been considered civil over time, there was Thoreau refusing to pay his taxes in protest of slavery, or Gandhi's hunger strikes, some of which lasted up to three weeks, in protest of the British occupation of India. There were the sit-ins that MLK Jr. coordinated during the civil rights movement, protests that began in February of 1960, when four black students from North Carolina A&T University sat down at a Woolworth's lunch counter in Greensboro, North Carolina, and grew to include twenty states and seventy thousand black and white participants in almost two years.

Up the scale from civil disobedience is a *riot*, defined by *Merriam-Webster* as "a tumultuous disturbance of the public peace by three or more persons assembled together and acting with a common intent." One might even call it an *un*civil disturbance. Most people count looting and indiscriminate violence to property as features of a riot. But a riot is also often defined by the race and class of people doing the rioting.

The American version of riots have happened for all sorts of reasons—people agitating for unionization, against Prohibition, over unemployment during the Depression . . . but the race-related riots that took place before the mid-twentieth century were usually white mobs attacking black people. In Wilmington, North Carolina, in 1898, a two-thousand-strong mob of white supremacists, armed with rifles and pistols, staged the only coup d'état on American soil: they stormed into the city hall of Wilmington, overthrew the elected government, forced both black and white officials to resign, and ran many of them out of town. They stomped through black neighborhoods, shooting black people, many of them unarmed, and jailed others "for their own safety" before marching them to a train and sending them out of town. They torched black newspapers. When it was all said and done, somewhere between sixty and ninety black people were dead.

We've already seen another example of an American race riot: the tragedy in the Greenwood District of Tulsa, Oklahoma. The mob of white men that showed up at the county jail, intent on lynching one black man, was fifteen hundred strong; about seventy-five black men, many of them World War I veterans, showed up to protect him. Violence broke out when a white man tried to grab a black man's gun and it went off. Many white people went home to get their own weapons. At the crack of dawn the next morning, thousands of white Tulsans poured into the Greenwood District, many who'd been deputized and given weapons by city officials, and spread out through the street, shooting black people on sight, as well as looting and burning more than a thousand homes (they even stopped the fire trucks from attending many of the fires) along with a school, library, hospital, hotels, stores, and churches. Historians estimate that, when all was said and done, as many as three hundred people had been killed.

Contrast this with the 1960s, when the character of the conflicts shifted from white people attacking black people to black people resisting oppression. White people still called that resistance a *riot*, but black people described it as a *rebellion*—defined as an often-armed resistance to an established government or ruler. Given that the police and racist institutions they opposed constituted an oppressive government, they reasoned, why should their protests not constitute a rebellion? This is in contrast to the supposed spontaneity of a riot, which implies that there's no motive involved, or there's an illegitimate one. A *rebellion*, on the other hand, implies that the actions are a response to injustice.

Riot or rebellion. For rebellion, think Watts in 1965 (where violence sparked from the traffic stop of a black man, and, over a seven-day span, 34 people were killed, thousands arrested, and millions of dollars in property damage occurred), or Detroit in 1967 (where after police raided a black speakeasy, a protest erupted that in five days claimed the lives of 43 people, injured 342 others, and included the burning of 1,400 buildings). Think of the small number of destructive and violent protests in places, including Minnesota (more later) and LA, during the Black Lives Matter movement.

Throughout all this history, white privilege has ruled how these conflicts were described. When it was white people instigating the violence, the media, politicians, law enforcement, and eventually historians called what was a massacre a *race riot*. When black people started to initiate the protests, the media called what was a rebellion a *riot*, a description meant to portray all white people (citizens, property owners, businesspeople), some of whom were in on the oppression, as persecuted victims of unjustified black anger and hostility, while also making white policing of the situation, no matter how brutal, into a heroic or at least justified response.

A note on policing specifically. When race conflicts have been instigated by white people, law enforcement has often responded on a spectrum from doing little to almost nothing, to deputizing other white people to participate, to being participants themselves. When instigated by black people, they have strong-armed protestors, arrested them, killed them. *The Washington Post* reported that eight people were partially blinded during a single day of the recent protests (May 30, 2020) by police tactics like tear gas. Over and over in the aftermath of black rebellion, law enforcement, predominately white law enforcement, has invested in more "law and order"—a decision, you might guess, that tends to make things worse.

Black Lives Matter (BLM) began back in 2013 when black organizers Alicia Garza, Patrisse Cullors, and Opal Tometi created a black-centered political movement in response to a Florida jury acquitting George Zimmerman of murdering unarmed black teenager Trayvon Martin. The movement really caught the nation's attention the following year during the protests in Ferguson, Missouri, over the fatal police shooting of unarmed black teenager Michael Brown. Since then, protests have been ignited all over the country, usually after the murder of a black person by a law enforcement officer—Tamir Rice in Cleveland, Eric Garner in New York, Alton Sterling in Baton Rouge. (Please look up these murders.) These days, the movement has forty global chapters and, as you've likely seen on the news, has been protesting against police brutality and for black justice all over the world.

What do you see when you look at the Black Lives Matter protests happening all around our world? And why do you see what you see?

One thing is for sure: there's still cause for Americans to feel aggrieved by their government. And at no time in recent history has this been more collectively acknowledged than during the protests spurred by the killings of George Floyd, Ahmaud Arbery, and Breonna Taylor, among others, over the last few months. *The New York Times* estimates that between fifteen and twenty-six million people demonstrated over George Floyd's death in the United States alone, making it the largest demonstration in the history of the country. Some researchers number the protestors at twenty-four million worldwide, which would make it the largest mass protest in history, period.

In Minneapolis, the city where Floyd was killed and where this iteration of protests began, protestors trashed a Target and destroyed plenty of other businesses. They burned police cars. Toppled other cars. Defaced buildings. People were beaten. And this kind of violence happened in major cities all over the country. Of course, there were many people engaged in civil disobedience, too, but the more riotous kind brought me back to my mother's anger at her sister's passing, to her banging herself against the wall. As the protests went on, though, I came to realize that even some of this action was coordinated, with solutions in mind. I saw people who'd been protesting showing up at community meetings and giving well-informed speeches about abolishing or defunding the police to reinvest the money in schools and community programs.

And I saw that all the noise was actually working. People started tearing down Confederate statues, which led to institutions taking down their own statues. Every company you could think of was making a statement on the importance of black lives. FedEx pressured the stubborn owner of the Redskins to change the team name. I'm in the book world now, too, and in a matter of a week, two black women were hired as publishers of major publishing houses. Heck, me writing this book came out of the unrest. The longer the protests have gone on, the more I recognized them as the dividend-paying rebellions that they are. The more I come to see the founders of the Black Lives Matter movement—Garza, Cullors, and Tometi—as present-day Sons of Liberty. Or rather, the Sisters of Liberty: women who had an agenda.

The 1963 March on Washington might be most famous for Dr. Martin Luther King Jr.'s "I Have a Dream" speech, but it's also notable because the march had a specific agenda. That agenda—or list of demands, if you will—was read by activist Bayard Rustin, the deputy director of the march, from the steps of the Lincoln Memorial. I list them all below so you can read them and ask yourself which of them, after fifty-seven years, have been met for black people:

1. Comprehensive and effective civil rights legislation from the present Congress—without compromise or filibuster—to guarantee all Americans: Access to all public accommodations, Decent housing, Adequate and integrated education, The right to vote.

2. Withholding of Federal funds from all programs in which discrimination exists.

3. Desegregation of all school districts in 1963.

4. Enforcement of the Fourteenth Amendment—reducing Congressional representation of states where citizens are disfranchised.

5. A new Executive Order banning discrimination in all housing supported by federal funds.

6. Authority for the Attorney General to institute injunctive suits when any Constitutional right is violated.

7. A massive federal program to train and place all unemployed workers—Negro and white—on meaningful and dignified jobs at decent wages.

8. A national minimum wage act that will give all Americans a decent standard of living. (Government surveys show that anything less than $2.00 an hour fails to do this.)

9. A broadened Fair Labor Standards Act to include all areas of employment which are presently excluded.

10. A federal Fair Employment Practices Act barring discrimination by federal, state, and municipal governments, and by employers, contractors, employment agencies, and trade unions.

The March on Washington, as you can see, had a whole lot of aims. As well they should have. Black people were in a bad, bad place in 1963. But looking at all the evidence I've been laying down, name one of those demands that couldn't be applied to the current state of things, too. The agenda hasn't much changed because, well, the plight of black folks hasn't. But hey—they didn't have the internet. We can do this.

Let's Get Uncomfortable

WHAT ARE THE sparks that ignite protest, riots, rebellions? Where are the lines between them today? And beyond that—what's *worth it* to create real change?

This is an uncomfortable conversation because it has to do with power and perspective. As I've been saying, there's often no difference whatsoever between a riot or a rebellion besides who's looking at it and labeling it. It's also uncomfortable because it involves the question of whether the only "right" response is a totally nonviolent one.

In the 1960s' civil rights movement, we had MLK and his nonviolent civil disobedience, and that was effective. But the 1960s famously had another civil rights leader: Malcolm X—at least, early Malcolm X, who preached "by-any-means-necessary" tactics in the fight for racial equality. The fact is, both kinds of protest helped to bring about that decade's hard-won change. I'm in no way saying violence is necessary to create progress—but I am saying it's easy to condemn the latter, and we also have to look at who is doing the condemning and how it compares to the justifications for protest in the first place.

As long as systemic racism exists, you can best believe there will be the need for people to protest it. Remember what they said in the Declaration of Independence: "In every stage of these Oppressions We have Petitioned for Redress in the most humble terms: Our repeated Petitions have been answered only by repeated injury." Protest, riots, revolts have been responses to repeated injury, and for what it's worth, none of them has gone as far as the response the Declaration is talking about (the Revolutionary War). They're also how some of the most healing, humane change has happened in this country.

This chapter's title comes from the late civil rights hero John Lewis, who had this to say about the fight for equality: "Do not get lost in a sea of despair. Be hopeful, be optimistic. Our struggle is not the struggle of a day, a week, a month, or a year; it is the struggle of a lifetime. Never, ever be afraid to make some noise and get in good trouble, necessary trouble." Addressing the hurt at the root of today's protests is going to take much dialogue and much action. Let's get in trouble.

Talk It, Walk It

THERE ARE SO many ways to fight for equality. You can march. Or you can write. You can sing, like twelve-year-old Keedron Bryant, who released an honestly killer song called "I Just Wanna Live," with proceeds to support the Black Lives Matter movement. Whatever you do, just make sure that you are sincere about staying committed.

What you can do right now is educate yourself on the history of civil unrest, not just in America but internationally. Look at what happened in South Africa to end apartheid; look at pro-democracy protests in China, at the Arab Spring movement in Egypt and elsewhere. I encourage you to visit the Black Lives Matter website (www.blacklivesmatter.com). Listen to their podcast *What Matters*. If you have the means, I encourage you to donate to them. Read *The Autobiography of Malcolm X* by Malcolm X and Alex Haley and also *The Fire Next Time* by James Baldwin. There are some great documentaries on protest or civil rights—for example, Raoul Peck's film on James Baldwin, *I Am Not Your Negro*. You might also check out *Let the Fire Burn*, about the 1985 MOVE bombing in Philadelphia, and *The Weather Underground*, about the radical activists of the 1960s. If you like hip-hop, try listening to some of that old Public Enemy. You could start with *It Takes a Nation of Millions to Hold Us Back*.

If there's a protest in your area on a cause you feel passionate about, model the kind of protest you want to see. If you have the resources, donate to one of the many bail funds, which help protestors get out of jail. You can find a national directory here: https://www .communityjusticeexchange.org/nbfn-directory. Look up the Google Doc created by Black Lives Matter activist Sarafina Nance, which directs people to meaningful places to support the movement. Find out if there are plans to build any private prisons in your state and oppose them. Find out if the police in your state are wearing body cameras (https://www.ncsl .org/research/civil-and-criminal-justice/body-worn -cameras-interactive-graphic.aspx) and/or if there are laws regarding cameras that have already been proposed.

Another thing you can do, and I hope you will, is help to get the officers who killed Breonna Taylor arrested. Go to change.org and sign the Justice for Breonna Taylor Petition (https://www.change.org/p /andy-beshear-justice-for-breonna-taylor). Send an email to the Kentucky attorney general (https://msha .ke/30flirtyfilm/).

You can also support efforts to defund the police. To clarify: defunding the police doesn't mean abolishing the police, though there are more radical calls for that, too. It instead means redirecting money from police budgets to other government agencies funded by the city. Defunding the police could mean more money for underfunded schools, for mental health programs, or for drug recovery programs, all of which can help to reduce crime. Before you say there's little chance of that happening and much less working, let me share with you that about a decade ago Camden, New Jersey—a city once ranked number one on the FBI's list of cities with the highest number of violent crimes, with a murder rate as high as Honduras—disbanded its police force and then rebuilt an entirely new one under county control, using a number of now-heralded progressive police reforms. Let me share that, after the protest in Minneapolis, their city council made a historic pledge to dismantle the local police department and shift that money to community-based strategies. Let me share that New York and LA have also committed to cutting their police budgets. (As well they should: the NYPD's annual budget is $5.5 billion, so big that if you were to compare it to other countries—yes, countries—it would make it the thirty-sixth-largest defense budget in the world. The *world*!)

We've got to think that grand. Finishing the work of protests in America is tantamount to finishing off racism. It's a big order: the biggest order. Which is why we need all the good people to fight, fight, fight injustice and inequality wherever we find it.

"So, my question is, on the daily, on the street, what is the best way for me to let someone know that I care? That I am an ally? That I feel their pain? I want to learn more and to help if I can. With sincerity, and compassion, and without coming across as a fake or with an ulterior motive?"—Michael

14.

YOUR PRESENCE IS REQUESTED

How to Be an Ally

I want you to know that in the last days and hours of my life you inspired me. You filled me with hope about the next chapter of the great American story when you used your power to make a difference in our society. Millions of people motivated simply by human compassion laid down the burdens of division. Around the country and the world you set aside race, class, age, language and nationality to demand respect for human dignity.

—REPRESENTATIVE JOHN LEWIS,
OP-ED, *THE NEW YORK TIMES*, JULY 2020

So, before it was *Uncomfortable Conversations with a Black Man*, I was going to call it *Questions White People Have*. As I imagined it, me and a few black friends would sit at a table with white people willing to pose questions about race, and we would answer those questions. I'd come up with this idea for a video series on May 28, just days after the tragic George Floyd murder. As it turned out, I couldn't get a group together—I live in Austin, Texas, and my friends are scattered all over—but, thankfully, I have a very close white friend who was all in. "Manny," she'd said (that's what my white friends call me), "we need to do something. I want you to know that I am here for you. Use me however you need. Let's do something."

I explained the video idea, and she's, like, "Sure, you got it.'" She drove the three hours from Dallas to Austin and dove in immediately. We went over the questions I'd have her pose—why are black people rioting, how come black people can say the N-word but white people can't, all the good stuff—we talked through everything, we rehearsed all day. My friend's mom is a history teacher, so we hopped on an hour-long phone call with her to discuss the questions and rehearse. My friend was staying at my house, because I didn't want her to have to pay for lodging or anything. We got Thai takeout, came home, and rehearsed more on a FaceTime call with her sister. Her sister was a little worried that my friend might look stupid as the white woman asking these questions, but nonetheless, we picked out an outfit that night. She went to her room, and I went to mine, and everything was good.

Obviously, both of us were nervous. I was nervous

because this could be something big and hopefully monumental. She was nervous because there are a lot of white people who just don't understand what's going on. She lived in Dallas, which was being rocked at the time by both riots and (white) panic about the riots.

I woke up the next morning nervous but still confident, ready to have this conversation. We were due in the studio by 11:00 a.m. At 9:54 a.m., I came downstairs in my house to find her with tears in her eyes, overcome by emotion. "I just can't do this," she said. "It's just not right. You should do it without me. They don't wanna see me. They want to see you. I can't do this."

So I did it alone.

If you've read this far into the book, I hope you are interested in being an ally. Or or are at least curious about what an ally really is. Or maybe you're wondering how you can prove you're an ally in more than words? Wherever you're at, don't worry, I got you. I'll give you my sense of how necessary allies are to the fight against racism and inequality. This fight has always needed white people in the trenches, and that hasn't changed.

Let's Rewind

WHY DON'T WE get started with a good working definition? This one comes from Racial Equity Tools (www .racialequitytools.org):

Someone who makes the commitment and effort to recognize their privilege (based on gender, race, sexual identity, etc.) and works in solidarity with oppressed groups in the struggle for justice. Allies understand that it is in their own interest to end all forms of oppression, even those from which they may benefit in concrete ways. Allies commit to reducing their own complicity or collusion in oppression of those groups and invest in strengthening their own knowledge and awareness of oppression.

The simple version is that an ally is a person from an empowered group who acts to help an oppressed group, even if it costs them the benefits of their power.

Now that you're an aspiring (never stop aspiring) ally, a little on the legacy you're joining. In America, allyship goes back to the white abolitionists, who, from the 1820s until the start of the Civil War, called on the American government to ban slavery. Arguably the most famous of these was William Lloyd Garrison, who became the head of the American Anti-Slavery Society and founded the abolitionist newspaper *The Liberator*. From the 1830s until the end of the Civil War, Garrison, at one point a close associate of Frederick Douglass, dedicated his work to the cause of ending slavery. A more radical ally was John Brown, the man who said he "knew the proud and hard hearts of the slave-holders, and that they would never consent to give up their slaves, till they felt a big stick about their heads." He staged armed rebellions including Bleeding Kansas and the infamous raid at Harpers Ferry, Virginia, which failed when the last twenty-five or so of Brown's men were overwhelmed by marines. (I am in no way advocating that kind of violence, friends, but we have to learn our history.)

As I've said, after the Civil War, the South developed Black Codes, which became Jim Crow laws. A lesser-known but no less dedicated ally lived in Jim Crow Alabama. Her name was Juliette Hampton Morgan. Morgan was a seventh-generation high-society Alabamian, who, while riding on segregated buses in the late 1930s, began to speak out against the unfair treatment of black people and writing op-ed letters to her local newspaper. That allyship cost Morgan her job and caused her much public and private censure. Morgan got a new job and eventually picked up her fight for the civil rights of black people—this more than fifteen years before the Montgomery, Alabama, bus boycott that helped kick off the civil rights movement. Morgan fielded threatening letters and telephone calls and had the mayor call for her to be fired from her second job. She became estranged from her friends and colleagues and even her own mother; someone burned a cross in her front yard. She resigned from her second job in 1957, and the day after she resigned, she committed suicide by overdosing on pills. The suicide note beside her said, "I am not going to cause any more trouble to anybody."

Since I'm an athlete, Peter Norman's allyship holds a special place for me. A little more than ten years after Morgan's death, Norman represented Australia in track and field in the 1968 Olympics in Mexico City. He won the silver medal in the two-hundred-meter sprint between two Americans: Tommie Smith and John Carlos, the gold and bronze medalists, respectively. Smith and Carlos told Norman about their plan to stage a protest during the medal ceremony by raising gloved fists in a Black Power salute. When Carlos realized he forgot his glove, it was Norman who suggested they split the pair and wear one on each hand. Norman also persuaded a fellow Australian teammate to give him a small badge that read, "Olympic Project for Human Rights," an organization that had been set up to oppose racism in sports.

Smith and Carlos were immediately sent home and banned from the Olympics. But they also received a hero's welcome from the black community once they got back to America. Norman was not so lucky: despite being Australian's number-one sprinter—his time of 20.06 seconds is still the Australian two-hundred-meter sprint record—his allyship got him ejected from the world of Australian track and field and branded a social pariah in his home country. Thirty-eight years later, in 2006,

Smith and Carlos were pallbearers at Norman's funeral.

A story of allyship that is also close to me is that of Chris Long. Malcolm Jenkins was a safety for the Philadelphia Eagles who'd been very active and vocal in his leadership around Black Lives Matter. Chris Long, a white defensive end on the team, stood by Jenkins. When Malcolm raised his fist up, Long raised his fist up or put his hand on Malcolm's shoulder. It's one thing for a black person to raise their fist. They've got a lot more incentive to do so. It's a whole other statement when the white person is standing there raising their fist as well. Given how the NFL has treated Colin Kaepernick, as well as Black Lives Matter protests in general, Long standing with Jenkins was huge.

Now that I've brought the history of allyship up to the present day, let me tell you what you don't want it to become. What you don't want your allyship to become is an instance of the white savior complex. A *white savior* is a white person who acts to help nonwhite people, but in a context that can be perceived as self-serving. A white savior is someone motivated by thinking something like this: *I have to save black people, because without me, they won't be able to save themselves.*

Don't let this be you, my friends. The white savior looks sexy in the movies, like in *Hidden Figures* when the Kevin Costner character smashes a "colored bathroom" sign—a completely fabricated moment in a movie based on real life—or in *The Help*, with Emma Stone's character writing down the experiences of black maids and gaining credit for an act of civil rights activism. Maybe the most famous of all fictional white saviors is Atticus Finch, the lawyer who defends a black man accused of rape in *To Kill a Mockingbird*. I know that book is close to a lot of you. But trust me, there's a real danger in centering our narratives of racial struggle on well-intentioned white people, one articulated well by writer Teju Cole in his essay "The White-Savior Industrial Complex." Cole writes, "What innocent heroes don't always understand is that they play a useful role for people who have much more cynical motives. The White Savior Industrial Complex is a valve for releasing the unbearable pressures that build in a system built on pillage"—a.k.a., a way for white people to say, "Look, the civil rights movement was great. Look, we love a good deed here and there. Let us stay in control; the status quo is mostly fine."

You might not be able to control the powers that be, but you can make sure that your allyship comes from a pure place. Do good work, but don't make the mistake of caring more about your intentions than about the impact of your intentions, or seeking out gratitude or praise. Make sure you aren't engaged in optical allyship—the kind that goes only so far as it takes to get the right post for social media. True allyship is a commitment to fight this fight for the long haul: long after it ceases to be a top-of-the-fold news item, long after the cameras have stopped capturing it. Not today, but tomorrow, next week, next year, next decade.

Let's Get Uncomfortable

THE CONVERSATIONS OF allyship start with the self, with those tough internal monologues. Here are some of the questions you should be asking yourself. How are you as a white person holding other white people accountable? If you hear a white person use the N-word, call them out on it. If your classmate is being treated unfairly, speak up for them. If you know the black person on your job is being paid less, call attention to it. Make sure you have white people in your life that are doing those same things for you.

True allyship demands that it move from conversation to action. And that action will include risks. This isn't the 1830s or the 1930s, 1950s, or 1968, but I won't lie to you and say it'll be easy. The risks might be something as small as a distant social media friend unfriending you. But it could be something more severe, like ostracism from an intimate friend group, job insecurity, public or private ridicule, friction with loved ones. There's the small, small chance of what happened to Heather Heyer, the ally hit by a car and killed in Charlottesville, Virginia. Know that when you say you are an ally, you are saying that you are willing to risk your white privilege in the name of justice and equality for marginalized voices.

I'm from Texas—the Lone Star State. But the truth is, black people can't do it by our lonesome. We need white people to take on the role of coconspirators, confronting the issue of racism and oppression in your own circles of influence. In the story I mentioned to start the chapter, when my friend said she couldn't do it that morning, I tried to encourage her. But in the end, she had a change of heart. I don't know what happened overnight, but I guess she was tossing and turning until 4:00 a.m., woke up, and felt differently. She and I have talked about it since, and that's really what it was.

But that didn't mean I didn't have to pick up the slack: after our chat, I had forty minutes to figure out how I was gonna do this video by myself. When I got to the studio, I put my head down. The videographer counted me down, three, two, one. I lifted my head up, I stared dead into the lens of the camera, and I began my nine-minute-and-twenty-seven-second monologue, which within two weeks of going live got twenty-five million views and led to the creation of this book.

What I learned from my friend's choice was that being an ally is tricky. She had done a lot right: she reached out, drove all that way, and prepared for hours with me because of her desire to be an ally. And yet, when I needed her most, when I needed her in that moment to just sit there with me and have this conversation, she couldn't do it. And though I've forgiven her, at the time that broke my heart. Black people don't have the luxury to have a change of heart. It might not have been the world depending on me, but I didn't know who needed my voice, so I wasn't going to back down. The lesson there is that being an ally means showing up.

Talk It, Walk It

WE STARTED THIS chapter with John Lewis again, with the last piece he wrote before passing away. Note how he made a point to celebrate those now demanding change for "set[ting] aside race, class, age, language and nationality." You heard the man—he wants you in the game, too.

As with so much else, allyship starts with education. Some books to check out that I haven't yet mentioned: *Fatal Invention: How Science, Politics, and Big Business Re-Create Race in the Twenty-First Century* by Dorothy Roberts; *The Condemnation of Blackness: Race, Crime, and the Making of Modern Urban America* by Khalil Gibran Muhammad. I also suggest the classic novels *The Bluest Eye* by Toni Morrison and *Native Son* by Richard Wright. When you're buying these or any of the other books, it would also be great to support black-owned bookstores with your purchases.

If you'd rather start off with something shorter, try Ta-Nehisi Coates's essay "The Case for Reparations," or France E. Kendall's "How to Be an Ally If You Are a Person with Privilege." Also check out Rachel

Miller's *Vice* article "How to Talk to Relatives Who Care More About Looting Than Black Lives," and Corinne Shutack's *Medium* article "100 Things White People Can Do for Racial Justice." She keeps her list up to date. Check out NPR's *Code Switch*, a podcast the covers the subject of race and identity.

Other ways to be an ally are, really, everything I've suggested in the chapters up to now. Take stock of your spheres of influence. Do you live in a white neighborhood, have kids that attend a white school, work with almost all white people, socialize with almost all white people? Change that. Attend a protest; see how it feels. You don't have to lead a march (yet), but participate, maybe step outside your comfort zone and join in the chant. Do your homework and find out which political candidates are supporting unjust policies. Oppose them. Try your hand at organizing— call a meeting, develop a list of tasks to address, delegate responsibilities, and hold people accountable for getting them done. Talk to your friends and family, even the stubborn ones, about race. If you belong to a neighborhood association group or something like Nextdoor (nextdoor.com), and you see anyone racially profiling a black person or a person of color, tell them it's not okay.

Finally, take care that whatever work you do is in counsel with black people. Make sure those people tell you the truth and that you commit to hearing them all the way out no matter how uncomfortable it might make you feel.

Remember, if you're reading this, I'm counting you as an aspiring ally. Starting wherever you are is okay. Heck, reading this book is a great choice. Every protest you attend, each time you stick up for a black person on your job, every person with whom you have a real conversation about race, all of those things are marks in the win column. The important thing is to just keep showing up.

"What is your vision for race relations in this country? Some of the obvious things, such as elimination of police brutality and systemic racism, are critically important, but are they aspirational? Is that the dream, or is there more to be accomplished?" —Beth

15.

BREAKING THE HUDDLE

How to End Racism

Interview with author and Nobel laureate Toni Morrison, *The Colbert Report*, 2014:

STEPHEN COLBERT: I don't see race.

TONI MORRISON: [chuckles]

COLBERT: I've evolved beyond racism. I don't see race. I don't even see my own. People tell me I'm white, and I believe them because I haven't read any of your books. [audience laughter] But can I, as a white man, understand the African American experience?

MORRISON: Well, you have to know something about rac*ism*.

COLBERT: But then wouldn't I be a racist if I thought about racism?

MORRISON: Perhaps. But more important than that, is [that] there is no such thing as race.

COLBERT: Really?

MORRISON: It's just a human race. Scientifically, anthropologically. Racism is a construct—a social construct. And it has benefits: money can be made off it. People who don't like themselves can feel better because of it. It can describe certain kinds of behavior that are wrong or misleading. So, it has a social function. Rac*ism*.

But race can only be defined as a human being.

SEPTEMBER 21, 2014. Picture me in my first game starting as middle linebacker for the Philadelphia Eagles. We're playing against the Washington Redskins at home, and there's a midnight-green sea of tens of thousands in the stands of Lincoln Financial Field. I trot out onto the bermuda grass, listening to the defensive coach bark the play through the headset in my helmet. I take a knee, feeling my heart pumping with nerves (it's only the third game of my second season), feeling the heat of my teammates as they wait for me to relay what to do.

You see, as a middle linebacker, it's my job to gather the other ten players into the huddle and call the play. Every single player has a responsibility, although what's called in the huddle means different things to different players based on their position. It's without doubt an important part of the game. But, see, here's the thing. Nobody comes to a game to see the players huddle. They come to see the players execute the plays that are called in the huddle. The way I see it, this book is like the huddle. I've announced the plays, and while the chapters may speak to different readers in different ways, the time is almost here for all of us to go run the play. Because, ultimately, it's not about the huddle; it's about what you do after you break.

We about to break, my friends.

Okay, one more story first. During the coronavirus pandemic, I've found ways to work out outside of a gym, and one of them has been biking. The problem is I haven't biked since I was, like, twelve, and I'm now twenty-nine. Still, I went to the store one day and got me a nice bike. My first time out, I was super excited to ride, extremely excited. I took it into the scorching Austin heat. I'd bought a little bike helmet to go with my new ride. I had my bike gloves. You couldn't tell me I wasn't a Tour de France winner.

I rode around my neighborhood, and everything was fine, just fine, till I tried to bike up a steep hill. I couldn't get up. I pedaled hard, but I just couldn't make it. So I got off and started walking. And then I took another lap and tried to ride back up. Once again, I couldn't make it up. I was determined not to let the hill beat me, Mr. Former Middle Linebacker. And then I saw one of my neighbors, and they were like, "Hey, you might have an easier time if you shift the gears." Um . . . why didn't I think of that? Well, I hadn't thought of it because, despite my fancy bike and all my equipment, I hadn't ridden a bike in a long time. I'd forgotten there was a gear shifter on the bike. As soon as I lowered the gear, I was finally able to pedal up the hill.

Is it even possible to end racism? I bet you've been wondering, and you're not alone. It's not an easy answer, but I think it involves looking for the gears we haven't used yet.

Long ago, plenty of people believed that slavery would never end. Before 2008, plenty of people believed it was impossible for a man named Barack Hussein Obama to win the presidency. The irony is that some of those same people hailed President Obama as the symbol of post-racial America once he assumed office. I never bought it; heralding a post-racial America was also like saying the work of ending racism was done, like we could take off our pads, hit the showers, and go celebrate the victory. And that work has never been done. Racism has been shape-shifting, and fighting it demands vigilance against its many changing forms.

Still. Though it's been with us for more than four hundred years and is as adaptable as anything I can think of—the fact that it was man-made gives me faith that we can still yet undo it. Not in our lifetimes, maybe not in anyone's lifetime. It's important not to let that discourage you but rather encourage you to stay in this long, noble fight.

Let's Rewind

ALL RIGHT, BEFORE we break this huddle, let's run it from the top. The racism I've covered in this book falls into three basic categories. The first is individual—the acts and expressions of discrimination, stereotyping, ignorance, or hate one person can level at another— and is broadly what we covered in part 1. The second level is systemic racism: the unfair policies, practices, and procedures of institutions that produce racially inequitable outcomes for black people and POC, while also yielding advantages for white people. You remember part 2. The third level of racism is a little different; it doesn't map onto part 3, rather it runs through and under a lot of the pain in this book. That's internalized racism: when people of color support white privilege and power, or when they're driven to doubt who they are, or doubt each other, or accept the status quo. This is everything from me as a kid wondering if I wasn't "black enough," to a formerly enslaved man seeking to buy his own grand-son, to black people who use positions of power to reinforce racist policies or attitudes. It is every bit as linked to the effects of white racism as everything else we've covered, and it is part of what needs to change.

I started this book talking about how important language is to black identity and how you should always strive to find the right language to identify a black person (I prefer "black," if ever we should meet). We covered white privilege, that invisible but ever-present advantage for white people, how it works like the benefit of the doubt, how it makes whiteness the default normal. We added cultural appropria-tion, which in America is, in essence, white people plagiarizing the culture of an oppressed group. Not okay—but also an opportunity to look for ways of engaging with and learning about other cultures without stealing or stereotyping. Speaking of stereotypes, we spent some time with the Angry Black Man. If you're a white woman, please, please don't be a Karen. Don't threaten to call the police on a black person for little to no reason. If you're a white man, don't literally weaponize your whiteness. And none of y'all better be using the N-word.

When it comes to systemic racism, remember that in America, it goes back four centuries to when the first Africans arrived on these shores and links up through the advantages still enjoyed by white people in almost every area of society—education, housing, and employment, to name a few. Recall that there's no such thing as reverse racism. Yeah, a black person can be racist individually (see earlier), but black people as a whole don't have enough power in America to effect systemic racism. Black people have had that power seized from them in a Fix secured by tactics including voter suppression and jury-rigging. Our biased criminal justice system works hand in hand with the stereotype of black men as inherently dangerous, as thugs and gang members—which leads to over-policing, over-incarceration, and yet more bias in the justice system.

Black people being murdered by law enforcement, specifically, is what led to the formation of Black

Lives Matter in 2013, a crusade to end policy brutality and achieve social equality for black people. In many ways, it follows in the footsteps of other movements in this country aimed at obtaining true freedom for black people—the abolitionist movement and the civil rights movement being two of them. In all of those campaigns, black people have needed white allies, white people who've been willing to take on the issue of oppression and racism as their own, even when it meant giving up some of their privileges.

When the first Africans arrived in 1619 in Virginia, there was no such thing as a white person. As far as the law is concerned, white people as a race didn't exist until 1681, when colonial American lawmakers sought to outlaw marriages between European people and others. Before that, people were known by their nation of origin, what we might now refer to as nationality or ethnicity. Anti-miscegenation laws, the laws prohibiting Europeans from marrying (and having children with) people of African descent, forged the white race.

Let's think about what this means: race was a political creation, an economic creation—all this hate developed to secure the interest of some seventeenth-century dudes who wanted to get rich growing sugarcane and cotton, who wanted to make sure they'd always be the class on top. Which is to say, racism has always been about power. Which is to say, we invented racism. Which is to say, maybe we can learn to uninvent it, too.

Let me tell you what the movement for racial equality can't afford: white people being fragile about racial issues. The premise of this book is about putting those issues on the table, about engaging with tough conversations, about white people having to sit with the discomfort, because that's how progress is made. This is not to say I want to intentionally hurt a white person's feelings. On the contrary, I want to move us toward healing. But we can't get to that part without the hard truths being a part of it.

If you are raising white kids, please, please talk to them about race. We must all see color to see racism. Plus, color and ethnicity are part of what makes people human, and to deny any of us our particularity is to deny our humanity. And, as Toni Morrison said, race is, if nothing else, human.

Let's Get Uncomfortable

THE HEART OF this book has been a conversation. Hopefully, as you've been reading, you've been having similar conversations with the people who are close to you, about race, about class, about politics. Hopefully, too, you've been talking to black people. Listen to them, even when it makes you a little squeamish. And if you find that you can't come to some agreement, disagree respectfully. White privilege can assert itself in conversation in a few ways, so stay wary. Never dominate the discussion, and try not to respond by reframing or reinterpreting what a black person or POC is saying. Instead of telling someone to "calm down" if they are, say, passionately recounting a racially charged incident, understand their emotion and work hard to hear them. And try not to refocus race-based discussions on other forms of privilege; for example, a white woman talking about patriarchy. This is not to say that other forms of oppression aren't valid, and indeed we need all the intersectional discussions we can get. It's just to say that the focus should be on the subject at hand. And also, this is not the oppression Olympics.

Some advice about facilitating group discussions. Make sure that you establish whether what's shared in the group is confidential. When you're talking, frame what you say with *I* statements, to avoid generalizing or speaking for a group. Figure out when to step back and quiet down. If you're normally quiet, you might want to challenge yourself to step up in a conversation. If you normally share a lot, you might want to challenge yourself to step back and do more listening.

Also, you don't want to tire yourself out in your rookie season or even your second or third. Pace yourself. At the end of this, you'll have a long career.

Talk It, Walk It

I WANT TO close with telling you about my friend Brittney. She's a white girl, twenty-seven years old, blond hair, born and raised in Austin, Texas. She's so different from me. Whenever I do something that just makes her shake her head, she always says, "Oh, *bless*," in a Southern accent. In return I'll usually say, "You trippin'." The truth is Brittney and I live life together as extremely close friends not only despite but in celebration of our differences—because I look at her whiteness, and I appreciate the beauty that comes with the person. And she looks at me, and my blackness, and my culture, and she appreciates the beauty that comes with that. We don't try to change the other person. We just smile and laugh with, and sometimes at, the other person.

As I think about what a country or world without racism might look like, I'm reminded of June 14, 2020. Little did I know that Brittney and one of my best friends, a black girl named Morolake, had conspired to throw me a surprise party. It was a party to celebrate me moving to Los Angeles to take my new job ("Speak For Yourself," which I was to cohost on Fox Sports 1). I was sitting at the house of one of my old producers at ESPN, Ande, just reminiscing on my time in Austin, when Brit and Mo called to tell me some weird odor was coming from my house. I desperately had to get back home, they said, like, fifteen minutes across town. I was like, "Guys, whatever it is, I'm not worried." But they insisted, "You got to handle this immediately."

Ande and I hugged and shed a couple of tears, and I sped home to investigate a mystery smell, which in hindsight really made no sense. I walked into my house and saw Brittney. And she was like, "Hurry up, come around the corner. Here it is." And as I turned the corner, I heard, "Surprise!"

There were seventeen smiling faces looking at me: all of my dearest friends in Austin wishing me goodbye. Of that friend group, eight people were white. Some were pastors, small-group leaders, strength coaches in Austin. And of that group, seven people were black. There were a couple of former current professional athletes. One person was mixed race, and another was Mexican. And they were all gathered in my house with smiles on their faces as we celebrated. Mind you, this was in the midst of shooting episode 3 of *Uncomfortable Conversations with a Black Man*. I realized that I was living out what I'm promoting on the show, and that was a great feeling. Because in that room were white, black, Mexican, and mixed people, and we were all there eating and laughing and talking and enjoying each other's company.

We were all also wearing masks since it was still during the coronavirus (2020, am I right?). But at one point, we took off our masks for a second to take a picture together. My aim is that life look a lot like the group of seventeen people gathered around my kitchen island with smiles on their faces, living life together at my surprise party. A world without racism is being in one country, on one continent, in one world celebrating life together, wherever we've come from to get there.

Ending racism is not a finish line that we will cross. It's a road we'll travel.

ACKNOWLEDGMENTS

I THINK THIS is the part of the book where I'm supposed to say thank you to all of the instrumental people who helped me create *Uncomfortable Conversations with a Black Man*. It's almost like an acceptance speech. Which, by the way, I've never been good at giving because I didn't really win a lot growing up, but here goes nothing!

To you, yes you, the reader. Thank YOU. This book, this project, the sleepless nights, arthritic fingers, and bruised vocal chords are well worth it because you have chosen to take a first step toward making our world a better place. So thank you for sitting at this table with me, for having this conversation, and for motivating me to keep going, even when I was tempted to stop.

Oprah, I can honestly say I never thought I would be thanking you in my life, particularly because I never thought we would speak or you would know who I am. However, I have quickly realized that good people are attracted to good things. Thank you for stopping what you were doing just to hop on the phone with me in the middle of a pandemic and hear my heart. I played team sports my whole life, and I can confidently say you're one of the best teammates I've ever had.

Mitch, the man who put his life on pause, dropping everything to help me make my dream come true. I'm glad you checked your Twitter direct messages that day, because if not, the world may not have this book. You're an incredible thinker, an incredible writer, and an unsung hero. Thank you, my friend.

Meghan, when we first met on Zoom and they told me, "She's going to be your best friend over the next few months," I was like, "Yeah, right." Well, yeah, they were right. You responded to questions at all hours, challenged my thoughts for the better, and interjected your pure and genuine, well, whiteness. You made one of the scariest tasks, writing a book, pretty manageable.

Meredith, it took you some convincing at first (don't worry, y'all; I'll tell that story in another book), but after you realized that the world could be inspired by my voice on this topic, you moved full speed ahead and made yourself readily available. Thanks for tolerating me and my madness, and thank you for helping this book come alive.

Terry, you saw in me what I hadn't yet seen in

myself: the passion and ability to take a positive message to the world. Thanks for believing in me.

Rachel, thanks for talking through this idea with me. After the murder of George Floyd, I wasn't sure what I was going to do, but I knew I needed to do something. When I asked you to join me, you were more than willing. When COVID-19 had other plans, you encouraged me and my ability to move forward even without you.

Taylor, you were right, "Uncomfortable Conversations" did sound a lot better than "Questions White People Have." This conversation went much further than we ever could've imagined while sitting at my kitchen table. Everything happens for a reason.

Mo, I'm forever grateful for you. You've been there through every episode of the show, and every page of the book. Before this was ever a book, when it was simply an outline and I had stayed up for twenty-four hours, falling asleep on the keyboard, you picked up where I left off and helped me make sentences out of gibberish. When I was too nervous to eat, because I knew the potential weight these words could carry, you made sure I was taking care of myself while attempting to help so many. Maybe this book could have been written without you, but I don't want to imagine how. Thank you.

To my brother Sam, you inspire me, encourage me, and motivate me. Everything I do, I try to do excellently because of you. You're my biggest inspiration, and I love you more than you know. Thanks for setting the bar so high, you've made me a better man and a better human.

Steph, your love for me doesn't go unnoticed. You've always wanted to see me win, and you were the first one to speak my current reality of life into existence. Thanks for believing in me before there was much to believe in.

Chichi, you're forever one of my favorite humans on the earth. When my life got chaotic, our conversations about nothing and everything all at the same time kept me sane. I can't imagine my life without you. You're the best.

Dad, I got my ability to communicate from you. The reason my words have resonated with so many is because of what I caught and was taught by you growing up. Thank you for the sacrifices you made for me, putting me in a position to try to change the world. You taught me how to work and how to sacrifice. You taught me how to deliver truth with grace and love. I am who I am because of you.

Mom, you're an angel walking the earth. If Dad taught me how to communicate, you taught me how to have compassion. Thanks for being my biggest cheerleader and biggest supporter. Thanks for always making sure that your youngest son felt loved and taken care of. I love you.

Lastly, I end this book the way I start every episode of *Uncomfortable Conversations with a Black Man* and anything I do of significance. By thanking God. I've consistently referred to this season in my life as my "Esther moment" (Esther 4:14). I'm honored that God equipped and called me to be a messenger in this moment. Jesus's love for me has set the bar for the way in which I'm called to love people, and the way in which I'm called to love you, the reader.

I'm humbled to have been able to write this book and facilitate this message, and I'm grateful that you chose to come on this journey with me.

Let's continue to change the world, together. I love y'all.

QUICK TALKS

IN THE NFL, you have a playbook, and your playbook has every play you could ever need on defense. Probably close to one hundred different plays. Different formations. Different variations. Different adjustments and so on. Week to week, you pick twenty to twenty-five plays from the book, depending on your opponent's strategy. During my time on the Eagles this always happened in the defensive meeting the day before the game, when my coach Rick Minter would hand out to me and the other linebackers what was called the *LB (Linebacker) Tip Sheet*. It was about twelve pages thick, stapled, your name and your number on the front, and inside, a reminder of all the plays we'd learned from that week, all twenty to twenty-five of them. At the very back of the tip sheet, the last two pages or so, was "things to look out for." These were things that may not have been what we had practiced all week but which you might see in the game the next day.

That's what this little bonus chapter is. There are all sorts of "things to look out for" in the road to anti-racist allyship, and also, I'm gonna be real, a lot of things I've gotten questions about that I didn't get to cover in other chapters. We may not have talked about the following topics at length, but I'm giving you this little tip sheet because you might see them in the game of life.

Terms

BEFORE I GIVE up the goods, let me say: everything I'll be talking about is a part of black culture. Me providing you with explanations is not about saying black culture is somehow weird, exotic, or in need of explaining. Black culture is not below white culture, and this isn't a safari. But black culture is, in many respects, different from white culture. And while you're reading this, keep in mind that white people have had the benefit of their culture becoming the mainstream. Black people have never been the mainstream, and whatever chances they've had for their culture to become popular, these chances haven't been anywhere near as long-standing or come as often as they have for white people.

As basic as it seems, let's start this dive into black culture with a quick definition of *culture*. Google the word *culture* and you'll find a whole heap of definitions, but for the sake of keeping it simple, I'll use anthropologist Bronisław Malinowski's description of culture as a "well organized unity divided into two fundamental aspects—a body of artifacts and a system of customs." Which is to say: cultures are things made by a group of people and also a way of doing things.

The second word I want you to have a handle on is *diaspora*. A *diaspora* is a dispersion of a people, language, or culture outside where they originally came from. So in the case of black people, the African diaspora includes black people and their descendants who are living off the continent. All black people in America are part of the African diaspora. There's also a white diaspora, too, though Europeans don't use the term as much. One important thing to remember is that Africans were mostly forced into their dispersion, while in America, the Europeans mostly came of their own volition (and also, of course, sans chains). Another important thing to remember is the diaspora holds a multitude of cultures. Okay, I hope that was clear and helpful.

Now to the tip sheet.

Black Names

ONE DAY WHEN I was working for ESPN, a colleague and I were on a break from shooting, and he asked me, "Hey, bro, I really would love if you just answer for me, like why do black people have the most unique names? Like white people, we have names like Steven and Dan or Sarah or Britney or Anna, but black people, you have Carmelos; you have LaMichaels; you have LeBrons. You have so many unique names." Well, black names are definitely a thing. But the first thing I'll say is that they aren't weird. They just aren't accepted as the mainstream.

To understand black names, we must be aware that during slavery, black people took on the surnames of their enslavers. We must note as well that while black people lost almost all their autonomy during slavery, many of them retained the ability to name their kids, that naming kids was an important means of establishing a black person's place in their community and was a means of keeping track of family members who were sometimes (often) sent elsewhere.

After emancipation, black people kept up the practice of choosing special names. However, the people who did it were always a small few, like less than 5 percent. Long before there was Latasha or LeBron or Shaniqua, there were Booker and Perlie. In fact, in the 1920 census, 99 percent of all the men with the first name of Booker were black, as were 89 percent of all men named Perlie. Names like Tyrone, Darnell, and Kareem were popping during the civil rights movement. According to an ABC News poll, among the top black names for women currently are Imani, Ebony, and Precious. Among the top black names for boys are DeShawn, DeAndre, and Marquis. Another fun fact about the evolution of names: historically, the more black people use them, the less white people use them.

Black Women's Hair

LOOK, I'M THE first to admit that I don't know everything about black women's hair, but I do know a thing or two. One thing I know is that for some black women, their hair is a crown. Another thing I know is that you'd better not touch a black woman's hair without permission. I mean, Solange Knowles literally has a song called "Don't Touch My Hair," and comedian Phoebe Robinson's bestselling book is called *You Can't Touch My Hair*. If you go to New York's famous 125th Street in Harlem and walk east to west, you're liable to see some black women, usually African women, sitting outside of a salon, calling out to women who are passing by, "Miss, miss. You want to get your hair braided?" There's a reason that these are black women who do this, a reason that you'll likely never see a white hair stylist doing the same thing. Because black women's untouchable hair is a huge part of black culture.

It goes back far. Check the ancient Egyptian hieroglyphs, and you'll see images of dreadlocks, Afros, and box braids, styles black women still use today. While twisted locks have roots in ancient Hindu culture, they are a huge part of African culture. In some parts of Nigeria—shout-out to my people—braids can communicate things like age, religion, whether a person is married or not, and where they stand in a tribe's hierarchy. And there are styles upon styles upon styles. The Bantu knots, which are big with the Zulus of South Africa. Braids are also an African cultural tradition that managed to endure while black people were enslaved. Like cornrows, which not only represented black folks' homeland but also helped protect people's hair while they were out toiling in the fields. Braids still serve some of the same purposes today. Plenty of black women wear them to protect their hair, even braiding synthetic hair to give it greater protection or for style. If you remember only one thing I've said, remember that many black women love their hair and love to style—and it's not for you to touch.

Durags

IF THIS WERE another part of the book, I'd tell you about how, up until the slave trade, many African men wore their hair long—it was a sign of many positive things, life experiences, social position within a tribe, and so on—and that when Africans got to America, white people, who were intent on erasing their culture, keeping their hair clean, and maximizing output, started making them wear their hair short. I'd tell you about how black men have gone through all kinds of popular hairstyles since emancipation, from the conk, to the Afro, to the Jheri curl, to the fade. If this were an earlier part of the book, I'd get into all of that history . . . but since it isn't, I'll get to the part I really want to talk about, which is waves. My waves.

Waves are the kink of black people's hair smoothed out with grease and brushing. And man, when I was a kid, especially when I was in middle school and high school, having waves in my head was like having the latest throwback jersey or some brand-new Jordans; it was like how it is now for a grown man to own a Rolex. To get waves, I had to wear a wave cap, had to slick my hair down at all hours, really all hours when I wasn't around white people. Well, the thing that I called a wave cap was also called a *durag*. No one truly knows who invented the durag, but a guy named Darren Dowdy, president of So Many Waves, claims that his father, William J. Dowdy, invented it in the late 1970s as part of a wave kit. Inventor credit aside, it's been an essential part of many a young person's quest for waves, as it helps compress them. It also evolved out of its practical means to become a hip-hop fashion staple (durag as fashion was never my thing, for the record). Dudes have worn them untied under a baseball cap. Or with the strings tied to the back. Or with the strings tied to the front. Whatever the style, there's no denying the fact that waves are an important part of the evolution of black men's hair, and durags are essential to getting them.

Sagging

WHEN I WAS in high school, I used to have to wear a uniform. And a part of my uniform was making sure my pants were pulled up on my waist and belted. At the same time, I used to watch people like Allen Iverson in the NBA, who not only wore his clothes super big but wore his pants low on his waist. That was the style back then, but my private school wasn't going for that, and neither were my parents. Now that I'm grown, I still don't sag—not my thing. But there's no denying that sagging is a black cultural phenomenon, the conversations around which are steeped in class.

What I didn't know way back when was that sagging came out of prison (maybe the adults did, and that's why they were so adamant against it). In prison, because they can be used as weapons or in suicides, belts are off-limits. Since prison uniforms aren't all that concerned with fit either, incarcerated humans have been known to walk around with pants too big in the waist—hence the sagging. Sooner or later, most guys get released, and those guys reentering the free world is how the fad of sagging caught on outside of the prisons.

Before long, young people were doing it, and their parents were admonishing them, which is a perfect recipe for them doing it even more. A word for the unwise who are thinking about taking on this particular aspect of black culture: sagging has been linked to hip and lower back problems and erectile disfunction. If that isn't enough discouragement, I offer you some words from the coolest president who ever lived. "Brothers should pull up their pants," said Barack

Obama in a 2008 MTV interview. "You are walking by your mother, your grandmother, your underwear is showing. What's wrong with that? Come on. Some people might not want to see your underwear. I'm one of them."

Personally, to my black people—you do you. And white friends, don't be saying otherwise, it's just not your place. But, yeah, I'm not gonna be showing my grandma my boxers.

Jewelry

ON THE OLD Kanye hit "Diamonds from Sierra Leone," he raps, "It's in a black person soul to rock that gold." Well, guess what: I wear my two gold chains religiously. You've likely seen a rapper (or an NFL or NBA player out of uniform) rocking their gold, too—likely with some diamonds. Well, as it turns out, black bling has a long, long history. Matter of fact, African jewelry dates back seventy-five thousand years to when ancient South Africans wore pea-size snail shells as beads. African kings have proclaimed their status with ample bling: gold necklaces, rings, bracelets. And it wasn't just in sub-Saharan Africa. Bling is a part of many African cultures up north, too (you ever seen images of Egyptian pharaohs?). Present-day Ghana was named the Gold Coast by early colonizers for the richness of gold in the area. And when I say early, I mean beginning in the 1400s with the Portuguese (followed by the Danish, the Dutch, the

English). Europeans arrived to trade for that gold and soon built huge forts to guard their treasures (that is, until they figured out there was bigger bank in buying and trading Africans). The Fulani have been known for their elaborate gold jewelry, sometimes wearing gold earrings five inches long. Ashante chiefs have been known for wearing gold headpieces and even golden sandals. Jewelry has had immense cultural significance in Africa. If you want to know why I rock my two chains or why Slick Rick has worn a bevy of chains since the '80s or why Diddy has worn a neck draped with chains since the '90s or why it seems like every young rapper today wears an inordinate amount of blingage, well, it's in our cultural blood and has been since before America was a thought.

Lotion

"WHAT'S THE DEAL with black people and lotion?" one of my white friends asked. I could've responded with the science again, told him that our skin acts as a barrier to the outside world and that it works best when it's moisturized. I could have told him that the deal with black folks and lotion is that black folks seem to have heeded this science more seriously. I didn't get into all that; what I told him was that dry skin shows up more prominently on people with darker skin, shows up as a whitish coloring that we call *ash* (picture the ash after a volcano). What I told him was that you don't want to be caught ashy if you're black.

If we call another black person *ashy*, it means we can see the dry skin, and it's a huge faux pas.

To fight the ash, black people use copious amounts of lotion, often carry lotions with them. I saw this video on Twitter the other day of a father getting his young son ready for school. The father took a big gob of Vaseline and spread it all over the boy's face. When he was done, the boy looked slick as licked Popsicles.

Vaseline is popular; so is cocoa butter or shea butter, or, in some rare cases, actual butter. What white people also need to understand, or not, about lotioning is that it is a cultural practice that is passed down from generation to generation. And this knowledge includes learning the spots on one's body with a high probability for ash: ankles, elbows, knees, and hands. Missing one of those spots leaves us open to teasing and/or to implying that we aren't taking care of ourselves. Neither of which is a good conclusion. So yeah, lotion is high on our list of self-care priorities. You won't get me out here ashy.

Black Don't Crack

ONE OF MY white women friends came up to me one day and asked me about the phrase "black don't crack." She thought it was just a figure of speech. Well, it is and it isn't. "Black don't crack" is like an anthropology and science quiz all in one. Per the anthropology part, when those early humans left the continent of Africa, some of them migrated to colder regions and adapted with less melanin (and other adaptations suited for colder regions). So goes the science, the darker your skin, the larger the pockets in the skin cells. Those pockets are called *melanosomes* and contain melanin. If you're pasty, you have very little melanin. If you're Asian, you produce a yellowish-to-reddish kind of melanin called *pheomelanin* (also the pigment behind red hair).

Black people produced the darkest, thickest melanin of any group. It's called *eumelanin*. Melanin absorbs and scatters more of the sun's rays, which means the more of it you have, the more protection from those rays. Any dermatologist worth their salt can tell you that there are two factors that cause skin aging: natural aging and photoaging. I hate to break it to you, but unless you've got a time machine, there's nothing you can do about natural aging, but photoaging, which is caused by the sun, well, that's another thing. The more protection your skin or some aid gives you from the sun, the better you will age. Hence the phrase "black don't crack" for us dark people. And if you're looking for the greatest example of "black don't crack," search no further than our radiant goddess Angela Bassett!

RECOMMENDATIONS

HERE ARE ALL my favorite recommendations from throughout the book (and a few more).

Read

BOOKS

- Theodore W. Allen, *The Invention of the White Race*

- Carol Anderson, *White Rage: The Unspoken Truth of Our Racial Divide*

- Jabari Asim, *The N Word: Who Can Say It, Who Shouldn't, and Why*

- James Baldwin, *The Fire Next Time*

- Eduardo Bonilla-Silva, *Racism Without Racists*

- Mahogany Browne, *Woke Baby*

- Robin DiAngelo, *White Fragility*

- Karen E. Fields and Barbara J. Fields, *Racecraft: The Soul of Inequality in American Life*

- Noel Ignatiev, *How the Irish Became White*

- Ibram X. Kendi, *How to Be an Antiracist*

- Ibram X. Kendi and Jason Reynolds, *Stamped: Racism, Antiracism, and You*

- Toni Morrison, *The Bluest Eye*

- Khalil Gibran Muhammad, *The Condemnation of Blackness: Race, Crime, and the Making of Modern Urban America*

- Dorothy Roberts, *Fatal Invention: How Science, Politics, and Big Business Re-Create Race in the Twenty-First Century*

- Cornell West, *Race Matters*

- Richard Wright, *Native Son*

- Malcolm X and Alex Haley, *The Autobiography of Malcolm X*

ESSAYS

- David Bradley, "Eulogy for Nigger"

- Jonathan Chait, "Is the Anti-Racism Training Industry Just Peddling White Supremacy?"

- Ta-Nehisi Coates, "The Case for Reparations"

- David Goodman Croly and George Wakeman, *Miscegenation: The Theory of the Blending of the Races, Applied to the American White Man and Negro*

- Langston Hughes, "The Negro and the Racial Mountain"

- Frances E. Kendall, "How to Be an Ally If You Are a Person with Privilege"

- Kee Malesky, "The Journey From 'Colored' to 'Minorities' to 'People of Color'"

- Rachel Miller, "How to Talk to Relatives Who Care More About Looting Than Black Lives"

- Corinne Shutack, "100 Things White People Can Do for Racial Justice"

- Tom Smith, "Changing Racial Labels: From 'Colored' to 'Negro' to 'Black' to 'African American'"

REPORTS
- Otto Kerner et al., *The Kerner Report*

- Daniel Patrick Moynihan, *The Moynihan Report*

Watch

- Ava DuVernay, *When They See Us*

- Sam Green and Bill Siegel, *The Weather Underground*

- The Hughes Brothers, *Menace II Society*

- Barry Jenkins, *If Beale Street Could Talk*

- Loki Mulholland, *Black, White & Us*

- Jason Osder, *Let the Fire Burn*

- Raoul Peck, *I Am Not Your Negro*

- John Singleton, *Boyz n the Hood*

- Bryan Tucker, *Closure*

Listen

PODCAST

- *Code Switch*

- *Therapy for Black Girls*

- *Therapy for Black Men*

MUSIC

- Keedron Bryant, "I Just Wanna Live"

- Jay-Z, "The Story of O.J."

- Lupe Fiasco, "Chopper"

- Public Enemy, *It Takes a Nation of Millions to Hold Us Back*

Search

- To find out about mail-in voting in your state: www.usa .gov/absentee-voting

- Polling stations in your state or community: www.vote .org/polling-place-locator/

- League of Women Voters: www.lwv.org

- NAACP: www.naacp.org

- Big Brothers Big Sisters: www.bbbs.org

- National Mentoring Resource Center: www .nationalmentoringresourcecenter.org

- The Marshall Project: themarshallproject.org

- Mashup Americans: www.mashupamericans.com

- Black Lives Matter: www.blacklivesmatter.com

- National directory of bail funds: www
.communityjusticeexchange.org/nbfn-directory

- Body cameras: www.ncsl.org/research/civil-and-criminal
-justice/body-worn-cameras-interactive-graphic.aspx

- Racial Equity Tools: www.racialequitytools.org

- Anti-Defamation League: www.adl.org

- United Nations: www.un.org

Do

- Speak up if you see a black person being harassed in a public space.

- Patronize black-owned bookstores in your area. You can find a list of them at aalbc.com

- Take an implicit bias test. If in doubt about which one, try this one by Harvard: (https://implicit.harvard.edu/implicit/takeatest.html)

- Visit the National Museum of African American History and Culture in Washington, D.C.

- Visit the Equal Justice Initiative's National Memorial for Peace and Justice (informally known as the National Lynching Memorial) in Montgomery, Alabama.

- Schedule a meeting with the diversity and inclusion officer at your job; find out about their initiatives, and ask how you might assist. If you don't have a dedicated officer, schedule a meeting with your manager or executive to inquire about the company's diversity and inclusion objectives.

- Join a gym in a predominately black neighborhood. I suggest asking for as many guest passes as you can to start, and if you are comfortable after several visits, try obtaining a month-to-month membership. It's a great way to meet black people.

- Volunteer at your local food bank.

- Take an ethnic cooking class. It's a great way to learn about another culture.

- Explore courses in black (or African American) studies, history, and/or literature at local colleges or universities.

- Sign up for a seminar in anti-racist training.

- Have some uncomfortable conversations!

REFERENCES

1: THE NAME GAME

Brooks, Gwendolyn. *Blacks*. Chicago: Third World Press, 1994.

Gayle, Caleb. "Juneteenth in Tulsa Is a Day of Joy and Pain. Trump's Visit Worsens the Pain." *Slate*, June 12, 2020. https://slate.com/news-and-politics/2020/06 /juneteenth-tulsa-massacre-history-trump-rally.html.

Smith, T. W. "Changing Racial Labels: From 'Colored' to 'Negro' to 'Black' to 'African American.'" *Public Opinion Quarterly* 56, no. 4 (1992): 496–514. https://doi.org/10 .1086/269339.

2: WHAT DO YOU SEE WHEN YOU SEE ME?

"African American First Names." Family Education. Accessed August 1, 2020. https://www.familyeducation.com /baby-names/browse-origin/first-name/african-american.

Edgoose, Jennifer Y. C., Michelle Quiogue, and Kartik Sidhar. "How to Identify, Understand, and Unlearn Implicit Bias in Patient Care." *Family Practice Management* 26, no. 4 (August 2019): 29–33.

Editors. "Eight Tactics to Identify and Reduce Your Implicit Biases." FPM. Accessed August 1, 2020. https://www.aafp.org/journals/fpm/blogs/inpractice/entry/implicit_bias.html.

Grush, Loren. "Google Engineer Apologizes after Photos App Tags Two Black People as Gorillas." Verge, July 1, 2015. https://www.theverge.com/2015/7/1/8880363/google-apologizes-photos-app-tags-two-black-people-gorillas.

"Minorities Who 'Whiten' Job Resumes Get More Interviews." HBS Working Knowledge. May 17, 2017. http://hbswk.hbs.edu/item/minorities-who-whiten-job-resumes-get-more-interviews.

Nieva, Richard. "Google Apologizes for Algorithm Mistakenly Calling Black People 'Gorillas.'" CNET, July 1, 2015. https://www.cnet.com/news/google-apologizes-for-algorithm-mistakenly-calling-black-people-gorillas/.

Rutstein, Nathan. *Healing Racism in America: A Prescription for the Disease.* Springfield, MA: Star Commonwealth, 1993.

3: THE FALSE START

Adichie, Chimamanda Ngozi. *Americanah.* New York: Anchor Books, 2014.

McIntosh, Peggy. "White Privilege: Unpacking the Invisible Knapsack." *Independent School,* Winter 1990: 7.

Taylor, Jamila, Cristina Novoa, Katie Hamm, and Shilpa Phadke. "Eliminating Racial Disparities in Maternal and Infant Mortality." Center for American Progress. Accessed August 1, 2020. https://www.americanprogress.org /issues/women/reports/2019/05/02/469186/eliminating -racial-disparities-maternal-infant-mortality/.

4: CITE YOUR SOURCES OR DROP THE CLASS

Avins, Jenni, and Quartz. "The Dos and Don'ts of Cultural Appropriation." *Atlantic,* October 20, 2015. https:// www.theatlantic.com/entertainment/archive/2015/10/the -dos-and-donts-of-cultural-appropriation/411292/.

Gray, Danielle. "Kim Kardashian Slammed for Calling Cornrows 'Bo Derek Braids.'" *Allure*, January 29, 2018. Accessed August 13, 2020. https://www.allure.com/story /kim-kardashian-called-cornrows-bo-derek-braids-lol -come-on-girl.

Horne, Madison. "A Visual History of Iconic Black Hairstyles." History.com, February 1, 2019. https://www.history .com/news/black-hairstyles-visual-history-in-photos.

Saxena, Jaya. "'What Would America Be like If We Loved Black People as Much as We Love Black Culture?'" *Medium*, June 2, 2016. https://medium.com/the-hairpin/what -would-america-be-like-if-we-loved-black-people-as-much -as-we-love-black-culture-c7bddee721c3.

5: THE MYTHICAL ME

Asmelash, Leah. "How Karen Became a Meme and What Real-Life Karens Think About It." CNN, May 30, 2020. https://www.cnn.com/2020/05/30/us/karen-meme-trnd/index.html.

Cassidy, Laurie. "The Myth of the Dangerous Black Man." In *The Scandal of White Complicity in US Hyper-Incarceration: A Nonviolent Spirituality of White Resistance*, edited by Alex Mikulich, Laurie Cassidy, and Margaret Pfeil, 89–115. New York: Palgrave Macmillan US, 2013.

Fottrell, Quentin. "How America Perfected the 'Art of Demonizing Black Men.'" MarketWatch. Accessed August 1, 2020. https://www.marketwatch.com/story/george-floyds-and-christian-coopers-are-all-around-you-just-the-latest-in-americas-long-history-of-demonizing-black-men-2020-06-04.

NPR.org. "'To Be In A Rage, Almost All The Time' : 1A." Accessed August 14, 2020. https://www.npr.org/2020/06/01/867153918/-to-be-in-a-rage-almost-all-the-time.

Westbrook, Dmitri C. "Opinion Editorial: Why Is It That so Many White People Fear Black Men?" *College Student Affairs Leadership* 1, no. 2 (2014): 3.

6: NOOOOOPE!

Bradley, David. "Eulogy for Nigger." *Independent*, October 28, 2015. https://www.independent.co.uk/news/world

/world-history/eulogy-for-nigger-the-provocative-title-that
-has-been-printed-verbatim-a6687016.html.

"How Americans See the State of Race Relations." Pew
Research Center's Social & Demographic Trends Project,
April 9, 2019. https://www.pewsocialtrends.org/2019/04
/09/how-americans-see-the-state-of-race-relations/.

Price, Sean. "Straight Talk About the N Word." Teaching
Tolerance. Fall 2011. https://www.tolerance.org/magazine
/fall-2011/straight-talk-about-the-nword.

7: THE HOUSE ALWAYS WINS

Adams, James Truslow. *The Epic of America*. Safety Harbor, FL: Simon Publications, 2001.

Armstrong, April C. "The Origins of the 'Ivy League.'"
Mudd Manuscript Library blog, July 1, 2015. https://blogs
.princeton.edu/mudd/2015/07/the-origins-of-the-ivy-league/.

Bouie, Jamelle. "Persistent Racism in Housing Is a Tax on
Blackness." *Slate*, May 13, 2015. https://slate.com/news
-and-politics/2015/05/racism-in-real-estate-landlords
-redlining-housing-values-and-discrimination.html.

Kijakazi, Kilolo, Steven Brown, Donnie Charleston, and
Charmaine Runes. "Next50 Catalyst Brief: Structural
Racism." Urban Institute, October 11, 2019. https://www
.urban.org/research/publication/next50-catalyst-brief
-structural-racism.

Menius, Arthur. "Country Clubs." In *Encyclopedia of
North Carolina*, edited by William S. Powell. Chapel Hill:

University of North Carolina Press, 2006. https://dev
.ncpedia.org/country-clubs.

Rothstein, Richard. *The Color of Law: A Forgotten History
of How Our Government Segregated America.* 1st edition.
New York: Liveright, 2017.

Simms, Margaret. "Say African American or Black, but
First Acknowledge the Persistence of Structural Racism." Urban Institute, February 8, 2018. https://www
.urban.org/urban-wire/say-african-american-or-black-first
-acknowledge-persistence-structural-racism.

8: SHIFTING THE NARRATIVE

Baker, Kelly J. "White-Collar Supremacy." *New York Times,*
November 25, 2016. https://www.nytimes.com/2016/11
/25/opinion/white-collar-supremacy.html.

Cottom, Tressie McMillan. "The Problem with Obama's
Faith in White America." *Atlantic,* December 13, 2016.
https://www.theatlantic.com/politics/archive/2016/12
/obamas-faith-in-white-america/510503/.

Desmond-Harris, Jenée. "Why We Don't Have White
History Month." Vox, February 7, 2017. https://www
.vox.com/identities/2017/2/7/14503144/white-history
-month-black-history-month-white-pride-nationalism
-racism.

Fish, Stanley. "Reverse Racism, or How the Pot Got
to Call the Kettle Black." *Atlantic,* November 1, 1993.
https://www.theatlantic.com/magazine/archive/1993/11

/reverse-racism-or-how-the-pot-got-to-call-the-kettle
-black/304638/.

Hauser, Christine. "Merriam-Webster Revises 'Racism'
Entry After a Missouri Woman Argues for Changes."
South Florida Sun Sentinel, June 10, 2020. https://www
.sun-sentinel.com/news/nationworld/ct-nw-nyt-racism
-dictionary-entry-revised-kennedy-mitchum-20200610
-427la6bndjevnpnblqclz5ptay-story.html.

Levine-Rasky, Cynthia. "The Practice of Whiteness
Among Teacher Candidates." *International Studies in So-
ciology of Education* 10, no. 3 (2011): 263–84.

Scott, Eugene. "Majority of Americans Say Race Discrimination Is a Big Problem in the U.S." *Washington Post*,
July 10, 2020. https://www.washingtonpost.com/politics
/2020/07/10/majority-americans-say-race-discrimination
-is-big-problem-us/.

Trainor, Jennifer Seibel. "'My Ancestors Didn't Own
Slaves': Understanding White Talk About Race." *Research
in the Teaching of English* 40, no. 2 (2005): 140–67.

9: THE FIX

Bright, Stephen. "Supreme Court's Ruling on Excluding
Blacks from Juries Fixes a Racial Wrong." CNN, May 23,
2016. https://www.cnn.com/2016/05/23/opinions/supreme
-court-black-jurors-bright/index.html.

Editorial Board. "Excluding Blacks From Juries." *New
York Times*, November 2, 2015. https://www.nytimes

.com/2015/11/02/opinion/excluding-blacks-from-juries
.html.

"Felon Voting Rights." National Council of State Legislatures, July 28, 2020. https://www.ncsl.org/research
/elections-and-campaigns/felon-voting-rights.aspx.

Garcia, Sandra E. "Texas Woman Sentenced to 5 Years in
Prison for Voter Fraud Loses Bid for New Trial." *New York
Times*, June 13, 2018. https://www.nytimes.com/2018/06
/13/us/texas-woman-voter-fraud.html.

Greenblatt, Alan. "The Racial History of the 'Grandfather Clause.'" NPR, October 22, 2013. https://www.npr
.org/sections/codeswitch/2013/10/21/239081586/the-racial
-history-of-the-grandfather-clause.

History.com Editors. "Jim Crow Laws." History.com,
June 23, 2020. https://www.history.com/topics/early-20th
-century-us/jim-crow-laws.

"New Voting Restrictions in America." Brennan Center for
Justice, November 19, 2019. https://www.brennancenter
.org/our-work/research-reports/new-voting-restrictions
-america.

Pilkington, Ed. "US Voter Suppression: Why This Texas
Woman Is Facing Five Years' Prison." *Guardian*, August
28, 2018. https://www.theguardian.com/us-news/2018
/aug/27/crime-of-voting-texas-woman-crystal-mason-five
-years-prison.

Stone, Tobias. "Five Acts of Voter Suppression That
Will Sway the Next Election." Medium, July 30, 2018.

https://medium.com/s/story/five-acts-of-voter-suppression
-that-will-sway-the-next-election-b6979e9ff94c.

Ura, Alexa, and Emma Platoff. "Crystal Mason's Ballot
Was Never Counted. Will She Still Serve Five Years in
Prison for Illegally Voting?" *Texas Tribune*, September 17,
2019. https://www.texastribune.org/2019/09/17/crystal
-mason-five-year-illegal-voting-provisional-ballot/.

Waldman, Paul. "Republicans Are Serious about Voter
Suppression. Here's How to Stop Them." *Washington
Post*, May 18, 2020. Accessed August 1, 2020. https://www
.washingtonpost.com/opinions/2020/05/18/republicans
-are-serious-about-voter-suppression-heres-how-stop
-them/.

X, Malcolm. "The Ballot or the Bullet." Cleveland, Ohio,
April 3, 1964.

10: THUG LIFE

Abdullah, Tahirah, and Jess Graham. "The Link Between Experiences of Racism and Stress and Anxiety for
Black Americans." Anxiety and Depression Association
of America. Accessed August 1, 2020. https://adaa.org
/learn-from-us/from-the-experts/blog-posts/consumer/link
-between-experiences-racism-and-stress-and.

DiLulio, John. "The Coming of the Super-Predators."
Washington Examiner, November 27, 1995. https://www
.washingtonexaminer.com/weekly-standard/the-coming-of
-the-super-predators.

Drum, Kevin. "A Very Brief History of Super-Predators." *Mother Jones*. Accessed August 1, 2020. https://www .motherjones.com/kevin-drum/2016/03/very-brief-history -super-predators/.

Garber, Megan. "'Thug': The Surprisingly Ancient History of a Racially Charged Epithet." *Atlantic*, April 28, 2015. https://www.theatlantic.com/entertainment/archive /2015/04/thug/391682/.

Hinton, Elizabeth Kai, LeShae Henderson, and Cindy Reed. "An Unjust Burden." Vera Institute of Justice, May 2018. https://www.vera.org/publications/for-the-record -unjust-burden.

Howell, James C., and John P Moore. "History of Street Gangs in the United States." National Criminal Justice Reference Service, May 2010. https://www.ncjrs.gov/App /Publications/abstract.aspx?ID=252603.

Lussenhop, Jessica. "Clinton Crime Bill: Why Is It So Controversial?" BBC, April 18, 2016. https://www.bbc .com/news/world-us-canada-36020717.

Mock, Brentin. "Where the Phrase 'Black-on-Black Crime' Came From." Bloomberg, June 11, 2015. https://www.bloomberg.com/news/articles/2015-06-11 /examining-the-origins-of-the-phrase-black-on-black -crime.

Smith, Troy L. "Stop Using 'Black-on-Black' Crime to Deflect Away from Police Brutality." Cleveland.com, June 23, 2020. https://www.cleveland.com/news/2020/06/stop

-using-black-on-black-crime-to-deflect-away-from-police
-brutality.html.

"10 Things We Know About Race and Policing in the U.S."
Pew Research Center. Accessed August 1, 2020. https://
www.pewresearch.org/fact-tank/2020/06/03/10-things-we
-know-about-race-and-policing-in-the-u-s/.

Washington-Harmon, Taylyn. "Racism Ruined My Mental Health—but These 5 Resources Are Helping." Health
.com, July 17, 2020. https://www.health.com/mind-body
/black-mental-health-resources-to-fight-the-harmful
-effects-of-racism.

11: PICKING UP THE PIECES

Cummings, Judith. "Breakup of Black Family Imperils
Gains of Decades." *New York Times*, November 20, 1983.
https://www.nytimes.com/1983/11/20/us/breakup-of-black
-family-imperils-gains-of-decades.html.

Delaney, Paul. "Kerner Report at 50: Media Diversity
Still Decades Behind." *USA Today*, March 20, 2018.
https://www.usatoday.com/story/money/nation-now/2018
/03/20/kerner-report-50-media-diversity-still-decades
-behind/1012047001/.

Goldberg, Joel. "It Takes a Village to Determine the
Origins of an African Proverb." NPR, July 30, 2016.
https://www.npr.org/sections/goatsandsoda/2016/07/30
/487925796/it-takes-a-village-to-determine-the-origins-of
-an-african-proverb.

Hunter, Tera W. "Married Slaves Faced Wrenching Separations, or Even Choosing Family Over Freedom." History.com, September 20, 2019. https://www.history.com/news/african-american-slavery-marriage-family-separation.

Krech, Shepard. "Black Family Organization in the Nineteenth Century: An Ethnological Perspective." *Journal of Interdisciplinary History* 12, no. 3 (1982): 429–52. https://doi.org/10.2307/203268.

"Media Portrayals and Black Male Outcomes." Opportunity Agenda. Accessed August 1, 2020. https://www.opportunityagenda.org/explore/resources-publications/media-representations-impact-black-men/media-portrayals.

"Media Representations and Impact on the Lives of Black Men and Boys." Opportunity Agenda. Accessed August 1, 2020. https://www.opportunityagenda.org/explore/resources-publications/social-science-literature-review.

National Humanities Center, 2007: nationalhumanities-center.org/pds/. Letter in Heckstall Papers (P.C. 582), North Carolina State Archives.

Ruggles, Steven. "The Origins of African-American Family Structure." *American Sociological Review* 59, no. 1 (1994): 136–51.

Tolman, Tristan L. "The Effects of Slavery and Emancipation on African-American Families and Family History Research." *Crossroads*, March 2011: 6–17.

Williams, Heather Andrea. "How Slavery Affected African American Families." TeacherServe. National

Humanities Center. Accessed August 1, 2020. http://
nationalhumanitiescenter.org/tserve/freedom/1609-1865
/essays/aafamilies.htm.

Wolchover, Natalie. "Why Do News Anchors All Talk the
Same?" MSNBC, October 1, 2011. http://www.nbcnews
.com/id/44740700/ns/technology_and_science-science/t
/why-do-news-anchors-all-talk-same/.

12: LOVE WINS

Bradt, Steve. "'One-Drop Rule' Persists." *Harvard Ga-
zette* (blog), December 9, 2010. https://news.harvard.edu
/gazette/story/2010/12/one-drop-rule-persists/.

Sussman, Mark. "The 'Miscegenation' Troll." *JSTOR
Daily* (blog), February 20, 2019. https://daily.jstor.org/the
-miscegenation-troll/.

13: GOOD TROUBLE

Astor, Maggie. "What to Know About the Tulsa Greenwood Massacre." *New York Times*, June 20, 2020. https://
www.nytimes.com/2020/06/20/us/tulsa-greenwood
-massacre.html.

Bisceglio, Paul. "There's a Difference Between Riots and
Rebellion." UCLA Newsroom, July 13, 2015. https://
newsroom.ucla.edu/stories/theres-a-difference-between
-riots-and-rebellion.

Boissoneault, Lorraine. "Eleven Times When Americans
Have Marched in Protest on Washington." *Smithsonian*

Magazine, January 17, 2017. https://www.smithsonianmag
.com/history/suffrage-civil-rights-war-and-puppets
-when-and-why-americans-have-marched-washington
-180961809/.

Buchanan, Larry, Quoctrung Bui, and Jugal K. Patel.
"Black Lives Matter May Be the Largest Movement in
U.S. History." *New York Times*, July 3, 2020. https://www
.nytimes.com/interactive/2020/07/03/us/george-floyd
-protests-crowd-size.html.

Gunderson, Erica. "Riot or Rebellion: Why Peaceful Protests Can Become Violent." WTTW News, June 1, 2020.
https://news.wttw.com/2020/06/01/riot-or-rebellion-why
-peaceful-protests-can-become-violent.

Hohenstein, Kurt. "Sit-In Movement: History & Impact
on Civil Rights Movement." *Encyclopaedia Britannica*,
July 22, 2020. https://www.britannica.com/event/sit-in
-movement.

Kelley, Robin D. G. "What Kind of Society Values Property Over Black Lives?" *New York Times*, June 18, 2020.
https://www.nytimes.com/2020/06/18/opinion/george
-floyd-protests-looting.html.

King Jr., Martin Luther. "Remaining Awake Through a
Great Revolution." Delivered at the National Cathedral,
Washington, D.C., on March 31, 1968. *Congressional
Record*, 9 April 9, 1968.

LaFrance, Adrienne, and Vann R. Newkirk II. "The Lost
History of an American Coup D'État." *Atlantic*, August

12, 2017. https://www.theatlantic.com/politics/archive
/2017/08/wilmington-massacre/536457/.

McGraw, Bill. "Riot or Rebellion? The Debate Over
What to Call Detroit's 1967 Disorder Continues." MLive,
March 12, 2016. https://www.mlive.com/news/detroit
/2016/03/riot_or_rebellion_the_debate_o.html.

Meese III, Edwin. "Crucial Difference Between Protests, Riots." *Grand Island Independent.* Accessed August
1, 2020. https://theindependent.com/opinion/columnists
/crucial-difference-between-protests-riots/article
_708dcc3a-b275-11ea-b732-836851efa8f0.html.

Meese III, Edwin. "The Crucial Difference Between Protests and Riots." *Santa Maria Times*, June 19, 2020. https://
santamariatimes.com/opinion/columnists/edwin-meese-iii
-the-crucial-difference-between-protests-and-riots/article
_503b6758-2653-5997-aac4-03a0f6b46bae.html.

Ray, Rashawn. "What Does 'Defund the Police' Mean
and Does It Have Merit?" *Brookings* (blog), June 19,
2020. https://www.brookings.edu/blog/fixgov/2020/06/19
/what-does-defund-the-police-mean-and-does-it-have
-merit/.

Waxman, Olivia B. "10 Experts on Where the George
Floyd Protests Fit Into American History." *Time*, June
4, 2020. https://time.com/5846727/george-floyd-protests
-history/.

Way, Katie. "How to Find Out Which Politicians Are
Financially Backed by Cops." Vice, June 3, 2020.

https://www.vice.com/en_us/article/bv8nj3/how-to-find
-out-which-politicians-are-financially-backed-by-cops.

14: **YOUR PRESENCE IS REQUESTED**

"Abolition and the Abolitionists." *National Geographic*,
June 21, 2019. http://www.nationalgeographic.org
/encyclopedia/abolition-and-abolitionists/.

Baker, Faima. "What Is a White Saviour Complex?"
Metro (blog), March 6, 2019. https://metro.co.uk/2019/03
/06/what-is-a-white-saviour-complex-8793979/.

Belle, Elly. "How White People Can Hold Each Other
Accountable to Stop Institutional Racism." *Teen Vogue*,
August 2, 2019. https://www.teenvogue.com/story
/white-people-can-hold-each-other-accountable-to-stop
-institutional-racism.

Borges, Anna. "31 Resources That Will Help You Become
a Better White Ally." SELF, June 5, 2020. https://www.self
.com/story/white-ally-resources.

Cole, Teju. "The White-Savior Industrial Complex."
Atlantic, March 21, 2012. https://www.theatlantic.com
/international/archive/2012/03/the-white-savior-industrial
-complex/254843/.

Garofoli, Joe. "Being a White Ally of African Americans
Means More Than Just Protesting." *San Francisco Chron-
icle*, June 6, 2020. https://www.sfchronicle.com/politics
/article/Being-a-white-ally-of-African-Americans-means
-15321365.php.

"The Harpers Ferry 'Rising' That Hastened Civil War." NPR, October 22, 2011. https://www.npr.org/2011/10/22/141564113/the-harpers-ferry-rising-that-hastened-civil-war.

"Juliette Hampton Morgan: A White Woman Who Understood." Teaching Tolerance. July 6, 2009. https://www.tolerance.org/classroom-resources/tolerance-lessons/juliette-hampton-morgan-a-white-woman-who-understood.

Kendi, Ibram X. "An Antiracist Reading List." *New York Times*, May 29, 2019. https://www.nytimes.com/2019/05/29/books/review/antiracist-reading-list-ibram-x-kendi.html.

Montague, James. "The Third Man: The Forgotten Black Power Hero." CNN, April 25, 2012. https://www.cnn.com/2012/04/24/sport/olympics-norman-black-power/index.html.

Morrison, Melanie S. "Becoming Trustworthy White Allies." *Reflections*, 2013. https://reflections.yale.edu/article/future-race/becoming-trustworthy-white-allies.

Lewis, John. "Together, You Can Redeem the Soul of Our Nation." *New York Times*, July 30, 2020. https://www.nytimes.com/2020/07/30/opinion/john-lewis-civil-rights-america.html.

Oluo, Ijeoma. "Welcome to the Anti-Racism Movement—Here's What You've Missed." Medium, March 2, 2018. https://medium.com/the-establishment/welcome-to-the-anti-racism-movement-heres-what-you-ve-missed-711089cb7d34.

Stewart, Emily. "How to Be a Good White Ally, According to Activists." Vox, June 2, 2020. https://www.vox.com /2020/6/2/21278123/being-an-ally-racism-george-floyd -protests-white-people.

Wang, Fei. "Hidden Figures and White Savior." Medium, January 29, 2018. https://medium.com/colored-lenses /hidden-figures-and-white-savior-771c49abbcd2.

Webster, Andrew. "The Real Story About Peter Norman and the 1968 Mexico Olympics Black Power Salute." *Sydney Morning Herald*, October 20, 2018. https://www.smh .com.au/sport/finally-the-real-story-about-peter-norman -and-the-black-power-salute-20181018-p50abm.html.

"White Allyship 101: Resources to Get to Work." Dismantle Collective. Accessed August 1, 2020. https://www .dismantlecollective.org/resources/.

"The White Southerners Who Fought US Segregation." BBC, March 12, 2019. https://www.bbc.com/news/world -us-canada-47477354.

15: BREAKING THE HUDDLE

Aptheker, Herbert. "The History of Anti-Racism in the United States." *Black Scholar* 6, no. 5 (1975): 16–22. https://doi.org/10.1080/00064246.1975.11413695.

Busette, Camille. "Mayors and Governors: This Is How You Tackle Racism." *Brookings* (blog), June 2, 2020. https://www.brookings.edu/blog/how-we-rise/2020/06/02 /mayor-and-governors-this-is-how-you-tackle-racism/.

"Can We Talk? Tips for Respectful Conversations in Schools, Workplaces and Communities." Anti-Defamation League. Accessed August 1, 2020. https://www.adl.org/education/resources/tools-and-strategies/can-we-talk-tips-for-respectful-conversations-in-schools.

Edgoose, Jennifer, et al. "Toolkit for Teaching About Racism in the Context of Persistent Health and Healthcare Disparities." Society of Teachers of Family Medicine Resource Library, September 18, 2018. https://resourcelibrary.stfm.org/viewdocument/toolkit-for-teaching-about-racism-i.

"Key Terms ~ Race and Racism." Vanderbilt University. Accessed August 1, 2020. https://www.vanderbilt.edu/oacs/wp-content/uploads/sites/140/Key-Terms-Racism.pdf.

McCammon, Sarah. "Want to Have Better Conversations About Racism with Your Parents? Here's How." NPR, June 15, 2020. https://www.npr.org/2020/06/09/873054935/want-to-have-better-conversations-about-racism-with-your-parents-heres-how.

McIntosh, Kriston, Emily Moss, Ryan Nunn, and Jay Shambaugh. "Examining the Black-White Wealth Gap." *Brookings* (blog), February 27, 2020. https://www.brookings.edu/blog/up-front/2020/02/27/examining-the-black-white-wealth-gap/.

McWhorter, John. "The Dehumanizing Condescension of 'White Fragility.'" *Atlantic*, July 15, 2020. https://www.theatlantic.com/ideas/archive/2020/07/dehumanizing-condescension-white-fragility/614146/.

"Racial Justice, Racial Equity, and Anti-Racism Reading List." Harvard Kennedy School. Accessed August 1, 2020. https://www.hks.harvard.edu/faculty-research/library-knowledge-services/collections/diversity-inclusion-belonging/anti-racist.

"Toni Morrison." *The Colbert Report.* Comedy Central, November 19, 2014. http://www.cc.com/episodes/4yp6vi/the-colbert-report-november-19—2014—toni-morrison-season-11-ep-11027.

Wijeysinghe, C. L., P. Griffin, and B. Love. "Racism Curriculum Design." In *Teaching for Diversity and Social Justice: A Sourcebook*, edited by M. Adams, L. A. Bell, and P. Griffin. New York: Routledge, 1997. 82–109.

ABOUT THE AUTHOR

Emmanuel Acho, the son of Nigerian immigrant parents, grew up in Dallas with his three siblings. He is a *New York Times* bestselling author and the host/producer of *Uncomfortable Conversations with a Black Man*. His groundbreaking online series, intended to drive meaningful dialogue around racial insensitivity and ignorance, launched in June 2020, with more than 80 million views to date.

Emmanuel is a 2021 Sports Emmy winner, Fox Sports analyst (cohost, FS1 *Speak for Yourself*), and television personality. He is a former NFL linebacker and has a master's degree in sports psychology from the University of Texas.

Coming in January 2022

ISBN 978-1-250-83644-1 (hardcover)

ISBN 978-1-250-83645-8 (ebook)